Creativities

For Kindergarten Through Sixth Grade

Creativities

101 Creative Activities
for Children to Celebrate God's Love

Patricia Mathson

AVE MARIA PRESS   Notre Dame, Indiana 46556

© 1992 by Ave Maria Press, Notre Dame, IN 46556

International Standard Book Number: 0–87793–485–1

Library of Congress Catalog Card Number: 92–71631

Cover and text design by Elizabeth J. French

Printed and bound in the United States of America.

This book is dedicated
to all those people who share
God's message of love
with joy and hope.

Contents

Introduction

As the people of God we are called to live our lives as followers of Jesus Christ through the guidance of the Holy Spirit. We are to live always as people of the resurrection, for this is the heart of our Christian faith. We are called to proclaim the good news to other people and to minister to one another in the name of Jesus Christ. As a faith community we carry on the work of Jesus and the apostles.

Each of us is called by our baptism to share our faith with others. Those who work with children have a special misssion to help young people understand that being Christian is living the life for which we were created. Our faith in God is not something that we can just hand on to the next generation. Faith is a process of formation. Children must be formed in and through Christ and walk in his way. This is a lifetime journey.

Each of us has unique gifts to share with others. We bring these God-given talents and abilities to our ministry. We are called to reach out to the children in our lives and to share our experiences, our faith, and our story with them. We must also provide opportunities for the children to share their faith experiences with one another. We must help children understand that God is what life is all about. We are called to be all that he created us to be. God is the source of our life and its goal.

The main focus of this book is helping children discover God's call in their lives and how they are to respond to that call. The activities described help children explore their relationship with God and with one another and bring alive the message of Jesus Christ so they can live it in their lives. The ideas help them understand that God calls us to a life with him.

Further, the learning activities and ideas presented here introduce children to the idea that we are called as a church to be a community of God's people; foster in children a hunger and thirst to serve others as Jesus did; share with children the wonderful stories of scripture so they can explore God's message; help children discover God's love through the world and the people around them; enable children to pray together as a community; and encourage children to celebrate their faith in God through the seasons of the church year.

It is essential in all that we do to remember that it is not our message, but the message of Jesus Christ that we share with the children. We must show love and care to the children in our lives. We must remember that God created each of them in God's own image and likeness. Each of them is a special, unique individual. We must always seek to know the truth of Christ's message. We are called to continue to grow in faith ourselves so that we can share that faith with others.

The learning activities in this book are designed for children in kindergarten through sixth grade. Many of the ideas can be adapted for other age levels. The activities can enrich almost any curriculum. Hopefully those who are experienced with children and those who are new to this ministry will find this collection of ideas to be a valuable resource for sharing God's word with faith, hope, and love.

Please note:
An asterisk by an activity indicates that the material has been adapted from an outside source. For full information, refer to the acknowledgments on pages 148–149.

Chapter 1

We Are Called to Be the People of God

Through the church we are united in faith and love with the Trinity — Father, Son, and Holy Spirit. We are called to be the people of God and to celebrate all that God has done for us. We are to live our lives centered around Jesus Christ. We come together to worship God and celebrate the eucharist. Then, renewed, we go forth to live as followers of Jesus Christ in all that we say and do.

The church today is one with the church of the apostles through the Holy Spirit. It is through the church community that what Jesus said and did is handed on from generation to generation. As God sent Jesus, Jesus sent the apostles; today we are sent to tell others the good news of God's love for us.

We are called to a life with God through the church. The church exists to point the way to Christ. The church stands as a permanent witness to Christ and a sign of his presence in the world. We are called as a community of God's people to bear witness to Jesus Christ to all people. We are called to live up to our baptismal promises by loving God and loving others in God's name.

Students in our classes need to reflect on what it means to be the people of God. They need to explore what it means to be a church community and what that implies for their own lives. We must help them understand that the church not only gives us a sense of identity as followers of Jesus Christ, but a mission to tell others the good news. We must provide opportunities for students to discover all that we, as members of the church, are called to be for one another and for all people.

Church Checklist

One way to lead into a discussion of the various facets of the church is to begin with a checklist. Distribute a copy to each student, then ask the students to check the phrases that best describe their concept of what a local church should do. A checklist can include various items such as the following:

A church community should:

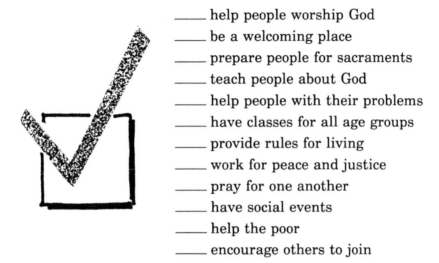

_____ help people worship God

_____ be a welcoming place

_____ prepare people for sacraments

_____ teach people about God

_____ help people with their problems

_____ have classes for all age groups

_____ provide rules for living

_____ work for peace and justice

_____ pray for one another

_____ have social events

_____ help the poor

_____ encourage others to join

When the students have finished the checklist, go over it item by item, inviting comments. Ask the students to explain why they think a particular item is important. See if there is anything that they think should be added to the checklist.

This idea broadens the students' concept of church and encourages them to learn from one another's ideas.

Action Rhyme

Young children need to learn that they are part of the church. The following action rhyme helps them understand that the church is not just a building, but is a community of God's people.

If I Were the Church*

If I were the church,
My church bell would ring,
"Come everyone," I'd gladly sing.
(*place hands together and swing arms*)

If I were the church,
I'd stretch my arms wide
To welcome everyone inside.
(*stretch out arms*)

If I were the church,
But I am, you see
For the church is people, you and you
And you and me.
(*point to others and self*)

The children enjoy doing the actions along with the rhyme. This is a good way of working with young children and expresses a concept of church in a way they can understand.

Church Tour

The church tour is a popular activity. Students of all ages enjoy an "up close and behind the scenes" look at various parts of the church building. This also offers an excellent opportunity to explain or review how various articles are used. The favorite part of the tour is usually the sacristy. Students like to look at the vestments and the bread and wine stored there.

Some of the things to see and explain on a church tour include the following:

Altar	Tabernacle
Cross	Chalice
Holy water	Paten
Baptismal font	Lectionary
Sacramentary	Bread and wine
Paschal candle	Presider's chair
Statues	Pews
Stations of the cross	Songbooks
Reconciliation room	Cantor's podium
Stained-glass windows	Sacristy
Ambo	Vestments

This is a wonderful learning experience for students. Many of them have never realized, for example, that the stained glass windows tell a story based on what we believe. Small tour groups are best so that students can see and hear everything. The students will remember the tour and what they learned for a long time. This is a great way to learn by doing and enhances learning about the church in a meaningful way.

Felt Banner

Banners help to remind us of the beliefs that we hold as members of our church community. Symbols on banners can express difficult concepts and may speak to our hearts.

Children can make individual felt banners as a craft project. Purchase precut 9" by 12" felt pieces at a fabric store to use as banner backgrounds. Fold down the top inch to make a rod pocket and sew or glue it in place. Scalloping the bottom edge creates a decorative effect.

Use additional pieces of felt for the banner symbols. Feature a prominent cross in the middle to remind us that we are to follow Jesus. Make the cross by gluing two strips of felt onto the background piece using craft glue. A dark blue cross on a light blue background, for example, stands out.

Place felt symbols in the four corners of the banner: the yellow sun represents God, the father; the green staff is for Jesus; and the white dove is symbolic of the Holy Spirit. The red heart reminds us that we are joined to the Trinity through God's love for us. Provide patterns for these symbols so the children can cut them out. The symbols can be arranged on the banner in any order the children like.

The final step is to put a wooden dowel through the top of each banner and attach a yarn hanger. The banners can be displayed at home as reminders of our faith and of God's presence in our lives.

Followers of Jesus

As members of the church Christ founded and bearers of the name Christian, we are to be a certain kind of people. We are to live as Jesus taught us. The Bible (especially the gospels) and church tradition help us to know what it means to be Christian.

Sometimes we need to help students focus on the type of people we are called to be as followers of Jesus. We may study various aspects of the church and Christianity in depth, but it is necessary from time to time to help students review their basic understanding of a Christian life.

Write the caption "Followers of Jesus" on the chalkboard, and then ask the students to contribute ideas about the kind of people we are called to be. Write the ideas on the board underneath the heading. It may be necessary to prompt students with questions in certain areas. For example, if they do not suggest any ideas about loving others, ask them, "What about our responsibility toward other people?"

Ideas include the following:

love God	help those in need
pray each day	respect life
share with others	take care of God's world
forgive people	work for peace and justice
love others	participate in the mass

Point out to the students in the class that these phrases contain action words. It is not enough to *say* that we follow Christ; we must *do* it in our lives. Ask the students to take a careful look at this list and see if there is an area in which they may need to improve. Suggest that they ask for God's help in this area, and that they work on it during the coming week.

Writing on the chalkboard like this helps prompt class discussion. It also helps the students follow and remember when they see the ideas in writing as well as hear them in class.

Sacrament Posters

The seven sacraments of baptism, reconciliation, eucharist, confirmation, matrimony, holy orders, and anointing of the sick are a means to life with God. The sacraments are celebrations of God's love and care in our lives.

The early church saw the sacraments as a continuation of the signs that Jesus worked when he was among them. He forgave sinners, he healed the sick, he broke bread with his followers. The sacraments are signs of Christ's presence in our lives today. Each sacrament is an encounter with Christ through the Holy Spirit.

Students who are studying the sacraments need the opportunity to reflect on all that sacraments mean for us as a Christian community. The sacraments not only strengthen us for the journey, but also help us express what we believe. Sacrament posters help students think about the sacraments in their lives, past, present, and future.

Divide the students into seven groups and ask each group to create a poster of one of the sacraments using posterboard and markers. Advise the students to include any symbols associated with their particular sacrament and label the poster with the name of the sacrament at the bottom.

This activity helps the students learn from one another as they work on their posters. The posters can be hung in the hallway as a source of reflection for all students.

Renewal of Baptismal Promises

It is important that students realize we are to live up to the promises made for us at baptism. We are to live always as children of God. It is helpful to allow the students to renew their baptismal promises at a paraliturgy. In this way they can make the promises their own.

Leader: *(light a candle)* Through baptism we became children of God. We are called to live always as followers of Jesus Christ with the help of the Holy Spirit.

Hear now the words of Jesus. *(read from Matthew 28:18–20)*

"Then Jesus approached and said to them 'All power in heaven and on earth has been given to me. Go, therefore, and make disciples of all nations, baptizing them in the name of the Father, and of the Son, and of the Holy Spirit, teaching them to observe all that I have commanded you. And behold, I am with you always, until the end of the age.'"

Children: **Praise to you, Lord Jesus Christ.**

Leader: Let us renew the promises that were made for us at baptism.

Do you believe in God, who is our Father and Creator?

Children: **I do.**

Leader: Do you believe in Jesus Christ who redeemed us through his life, death, and resurrection?

Children: **I do.**

Leader: Do you believe in the Holy Spirit who is present in the church and in our hearts?

Children: **I do.**

Leader: This is the faith into which we have been baptized. As a sign of your faith, please come forward to be signed with the cross of Jesus Christ. *(children come forward to have the sign of the cross made on their foreheads with holy water)* God bless you Father, Son, and Holy Spirit.

Children: **Amen.**

Leader: May we live always as children of God and followers of Jesus Christ. Let us now ask God's help to live as members of his family.

May we hear God's call in our lives and answer him.

Children: **Lord, hear our prayer.**

Leader: May we live always as faithful followers of Jesus Christ.

Children: **Lord, hear our prayer.**

Leader: May we follow the command of Jesus to love God and love others in his name.

Children: **Lord, hear our prayer.**

Leader: May we proclaim the good news to all people with the help of the Holy Spirit.

Children: **Lord, hear our prayer.**

Leader: May we now go forward to love God and love others as Jesus taught us.

Children: **Amen.**

This type of paraliturgy is a wonderful opportunity for growth in faith. It helps the children understand their identity as Christians.

Christian Recipe

As people of the church that Jesus founded, we are to be the kind of people Jesus showed us how to be. We are to live our lives so that others can see what being a Christian means. Jesus said that people would know his followers by their love for one another. We who call ourselves Christian should try always to live our lives as a witness to his teachings.

Encourage the children to think about what being a Christian means and then to create a Christian recipe for living. Such a recipe calls for a list of ingredients and mixing instructions, as does a food recipe. Explain this idea to the children and let them use their imaginations and their understanding of a Christian life to create a recipe. Below is a sample.

Christian Recipe

4 cups love
2 cups faith
1 1/2 cups hope
3 tbsp. understanding
1 tsp. forgiveness
Dash compassion

Mix together well. Serve with friendship.

The students' recipes will differ depending upon the ingredients they think of and the quantities in their recipe.

This writing exercise is an interesting way for children to reflect on what being a Christian is all about. It is a novel idea that makes learning fun. The students find it interesting to compare their recipes with those of others in the class and to see what ingredients each person thinks is important.

Mosaic Cross

Throughout the history of the church the cross has been a symbol of faith. We display crosses in our churches, our classrooms, and our homes. The cross reminds us that God loved us so much that he sent his only Son to us. Because of the death of Jesus Christ on the cross and his resurrection, we all have new life. So the cross is a sign of hope and love for Christians.

Students can make a mosaic cross as a sign of their belief in Jesus Christ. They need only construction paper, glue, scissors, and a little creativity.

Have each student choose one piece of construction paper for the background. Then the students cut out small squares from various colors of construction paper. No measuring is needed; the variety of sizes adds to the effect of the final project. The choice of colors is up to each student.

Show the students how to arrange the squares on the background sheet in the outline of a cross. Classes that have been studying various cross shapes used throughout the centuries will have a wide variety of choices. The students should be satisfied with the arrangement of the cross before gluing. Glue sticks work well with paper crafts and do not soak through the paper. This gives the student more control and the project a more finished look.

Each mosaic cross will be individual because of the different color and shape arrangements. No words are needed since the cross symbol speaks to each of us of our heritage as Christians. The crosses make a bright and colorful hallway display outside the classroom.

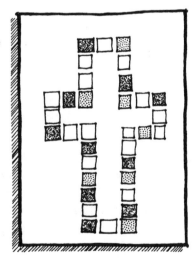

Saint Folder

The saints include many different types of people who answered God's call. All of us are called to be saints, to follow Jesus in the individual circumstances of our lives. We are to live the gospel message and share the good news with others.

Children need examples of how Christianity can be lived out in our lives. The saints are very important models. Through the saints we can help students become familiar with a variety of different ways to follow Jesus. The life of a particular saint can be studied each month, for example.

It is helpful for students to keep a saint folder. This contains all the information about the various saints they study throughout the year. A colorful folder with pockets is good for this project. Each student should label his or her saint folder and decorate the cover to make it attractive. Be sure the students include their name in case the folder is misplaced. Since everything about the saints is collected in one place, it is easy for the students to look through and review the material.

Information for this folder can include handouts on the lives of the saints, activity sheets, crossword puzzles, brochures on the work of religious orders founded by saints, word searches, prayers of saints, and other material related to the lives of these holy people. The following saints, as well as many others, are interesting to children:

SEPTEMBER 8. *Mary.*
On this date we celebrate Mary's birthday. It is one of several days that we honor her. Mary said yes to God when he asked her to be the mother of Jesus. Mary is honored as the mother of us all.

OCTOBER 4. *Francis of Assisi.*
Children find in St. Francis a saint they can understand. He loved God and all creation. Francis travelled around and told people about God's love for them. He called himself Brother Francis because we are all brothers and sisters in Christ.

NOVEMBER 18. *Rose Philippine Duchesne.*
Rose Duchesne was born in France but came to the United States as a missionary. Her dream was to work among the Indians, but she

was sent to Missouri where she founded a school. When she was in her 70s she was finally able to work among the Indians in Kansas.

DECEMBER 6. *Nicholas.*
Nicholas was a bishop who helped people in need. He gave away money to the poor in secret. Today we still give gifts in his name. He is known as the patron saint of children everywhere.

JANUARY 31. *John Bosco.*
John Bosco cared deeply about young people, especially those who were neglected or in trouble. He learned to juggle and do tricks to draw people's attention so he could tell them about God. He became a priest and also founded a school for boys.

FEBRUARY 10. *Scholastica.*
This saint had a twin brother, Benedict, who also became a saint. Scholastica established a religious community for women. She was a person of prayer who loved God.

MARCH 19. *Joseph.*
Joseph was the husband of Mary and the foster father of Jesus. He was a good man and did as God asked. He always trusted God. St. Joseph is known as the patron of the dying, because he probably died at home with Mary and Jesus near him.

APRIL 29. *Catherine of Siena.*
Catherine was not afraid to speak her mind. She was a saint of great determination and worked tirelessly for unity in the church. She is also known for the many letters she wrote in her quest to bring peace to a troubled church.

MAY 15. *Isidore.*
Isidore is the patron of farmers and rural communities. He was a prayerful person, who talked to God as he walked behind the plow tilling the fields.

JUNE 13. *Anthony of Padua.*
Anthony was a priest and a preacher. People came from far and wide to hear him preach the gospel. His words touched their hearts and gave them hope.

JULY 4. *Elizabeth of Portugal.*
Elizabeth was a queen, a wife, and a mother. She was concerned for the poor and sick in Portugal and tried to help them. Elizabeth followed Jesus' command to love others.

AUGUST 11. *Clare.*
Clare's life followed the model of St. Francis, who was her friend.
Clare left home to live a simple life. Her followers today still pray for
the needs of other people.

Many other saints can be included. The parish patron saint, for
example, should be familiar to the children. Saints are important
Christian heroes for children. Their lives help children understand
what it means to follow Jesus.

Feast Day Card

When a parish church or school is staffed by a religious order of priests, brothers, or sisters, there is usually a celebration of the founder's feast day. Making feast day cards helps children become involved in the celebration.

Cards can be made out of paper folded in half and decorated with markers. On the front the children print, "Happy Feast Day." Inside they print a greeting, such as "Best wishes on the feast of St. _____" and sign their name. Drawings on the cards make them visually appealing. Ideas for words and illustrations should be left to the creativity of each child.

Present the completed feast day cards to the pastor, principal, or a member of the order founded by the saint whose day is being celebrated. This activity both involves the children and pleases the recipients of the delightful cards.

This idea could also be used for the parish patron saint if the church is not associated with any particular religious order. Make the cards on that saint's feast day and present them during the parish celebration.

This activity helps students recognize the importance of saints in our lives.

Fish Mural

We are called by Jesus to follow him. Those who were first called by Jesus — Peter, Andrew, James, and John — were fishermen by trade. Jesus told them to be fishers of people; that is they were to help others hear the call of Jesus in their lives.

The letters in the Greek word for fish form an acronym, since each letter in this word is the beginning letter of another word. The words spelled out are "Jesus Christ, God's Son, Savior." The fish symbol became widely used as a symbol for Christians. It was used by early Christians secretly to identify themselves to one another when they were afraid of persecution. Today this symbol is still displayed.

One way to help children understand that they too are called by Jesus is a fish mural. This can be done on butcher paper for a large group or on posterboard if the number is small. Title the top of the mural "We Are Called" in large letters. Use blue tempera paint or a blue marker to draw waves across the mural horizontally. Have each child cut out a colorful paper fish from construction paper and put his or her name on it. Then the student glues the fish to the mural.

This project is a good class project since all the children contribute to it. The mural reinforces the idea that we are a community of God's people.

Light of the World

Part of being a member of the church is celebrating with one another. We are to remember that other people look to our lives to see what the church is all about. We are to spread the good news to others. We are called to ask God's help in everything we do and to pray together as a community. The following prayer service can be used by an individual class. Children should read the parts of the readers.

Celebrating and Serving*

Call to Worship

Presider: The community of the church is a light to the world.

All: **We are the light of the world.**

Presider: Every member of the church is called to live a good life.

All: **We are the light of the world.**

Presider: In this way, all people can see the true way to God and happiness.

All: **We are the light of the world.**

Opening Prayer

Presider: God our Creator, your Son Jesus told us that we must be the light of the world. Help us to show your light to the world by showing your love to one another. We ask this through Christ, our Lord.

All: **Amen. We are the light of the world.**

Introduction to Reading

Presider: Jesus taught us a lesson in this story by showing us how we can be a light to the people and the world around us.

(reading from Matthew 5:14–16)

We are the light of the world by the light we receive from Jesus. Let us think about ways we can share the light of Jesus' love for others.

Reader 1:	Lord, even when we are in darkness, shine out in our lives.
All:	**We are the light of the world.**
Reader 2:	Lord, even when we try to hide ourselves from you or from each other, shine out from our hearts.
All:	**We are the light of the world.**
Reader 3:	Lord, help us always to be sources of light to others.
All:	**We are the light of the world.**

Closing Prayer

Presider:	God, the Creator of light, you ask us to be the light of the world. Help us to be that light by acting as Jesus did with all those whom we meet. We ask this through Jesus Christ, your Son.
All:	**Amen. We are the light of the world.**

This type of prayer service helps to remind the students that it is Jesus Christ who is the focus and reason for our lives. It is he whom we serve through his church.

Mass Booklet

Through the mass we give praise to God, our Father, through his Son, Jesus, with the help of the Holy Spirit. We are to be a people of the eucharist, who live it in our lives. Studying the mass is important so that students will be able to participate more fully. The more children understand about the mass the more they will be able to use it as a means of worshipping God in their lives.

One way to help students organize their study of the mass is to help them make mass booklets. Use sheets of colored paper for the front and back covers of the booklets. Have them write "My Mass Book" and their name on the front. Secure the cover and other pages with brads.

The inside pages can include the following:

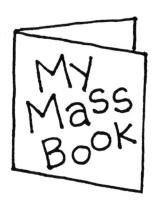

An outline of the main parts of the mass

A matching page of mass responses

A worksheet on scripture

A page of petitions

The words of consecration

A "fill in the blank" sheet of the Our Father

An activity sheet on the final blessing

The students can add original artwork throughout the book to illustrate what the mass means to us as Christians. This booklet helps the children organize their ideas and can be used as a reference later.

Children's Liturgies

Children need to worship God in a way that they can understand. Liturgies adapted for children help them to grow in understanding of what the mass means. Children's liturgies lead to a fuller and deeper participation in parish liturgies as the children grow and mature. Be sure to follow guidelines for children's liturgies in planning and organizing such masses.

The children themselves should take an active part in these liturgies. Roles for children include cross bearer, book bearer, lector for the first reading, readers of petitions (one child for each petition), and gift bearers. Children may also participate in the presentation of the gifts by bringing forward a special offering, such as food for those in need.

Use the readings specified for the day, but read from a children's lectionary; also use the eucharistic prayer for children. It is helpful to have a focus for each liturgy based on the readings which ties everything together for the children. The homily can develop this focus for the children.

Music is a very important part of children's liturgies. Sing songs that appeal to children and help them express glory and praise to God. Songs with motions are especially popular and meaningful for children.

Carefully planned liturgies can help students understand the mass and its importance. Children's liturgies can help children express to God what is in their hearts in a joyful and meaningful way.

Chapter 2

We Are Called
to Serve Others

Jesus came to reveal the Father's love for us. We are called to share that love with others. When Jesus was asked which was the greatest commandment, he said that it was to love God and love others. This is what we are to do as Christians. We are called to serve others as Jesus did.

Jesus Christ showed us how we are capable of living. He showed us the life for which we were created from the beginning. Jesus lived each day the message that he taught. He lived a life of mercy and compassion. He loved all people. The gospels are full of examples of Jesus' concern for the ill, the outcast, and the poor. He reminded us that each of us is created in the image and likeness of God. Each of us is called to a life with God.

For Jesus, love was a way of life and the center of his message. In the parable of the Good Samaritan he shows us that we are to go beyond conventional limits of caring. We are to love all people, even our enemies. We cannot use the law to limit our responsibilities. We are to care about all people in Jesus' name. We are to live out this parable in our everyday human experiences. We are challenged to re-evaluate what a life with God is all about. Jesus taught a way of life rather than a set of rules; we are to move beyond regulations to love. We are to have compassion for all people.

The law of love is dictated by the needs of others. It cuts across cultural and other manmade barriers. We are to help even our enemies and those who cannot or will not repay us. We are to work for the rights and dignity of all people. We are called to work for peace and justice. We are to follow God's will in our lives rather than conventional standards. We are to look beyond the externals to see the person made in the image of God. Jesus challenges us to live as God created us to live. God calls us to love others as Jesus did. We are to see Christ in others.

We must help students reflect on Jesus' law of love and its meaning in their lives. We must provide opportunities for service so that children can learn how to help others. It is essential that students understand that as followers of Jesus we are called to care about all people.

Message of Love

Jesus taught us that we are to love God and love others. This is what being a Christian is all about. Students must understand that we are to live this commandment in our lives in the way we treat one another. One way to help them become familiar with sayings of Jesus about loving other people is to have them look up and discuss specific Bible verses.

Divide the students into groups of three. Then give each group the following list of Bible verse references without the words. Ask them to look up the verses and write them down.

After they have looked up the verses, ask the students to discuss within their group how they can live the message in our world today. If possible, have adults act as facilitators for this discussion.

Following are some verses that can be used for discussion by the students:

Luke 10:27:   You shall love the Lord, your God, with all your heart, with all your being, with all your strength, and with all your mind, and your neighbor as yourself.

Matthew 25:40:   Whatever you did for one of these least brothers of mine, you did for me.

John 13:35:   This is how all will know that you are my disciples, if you have love for one another.

Matthew 5:44:   Love your enemies, and pray for those who persecute you.

Mark 10:21:   Go, sell what you have, and give to the poor and you will have treasure in heaven.

This exercise helps the students become more aware of their call to care about others. It also gives them the opportunity to review some important teachings of Jesus about our relationship with other people. Finally, the students also learn from the ideas of the other students in their group, and this provides added insight into what it means to live as Christians.

Caring Actions

As followers of Jesus Christ we are to be a community of people who care about others. Young children need to be made aware of ways in which they can help other people. Caring is a way of life for all those who call themselves Christians.

Initiate a class discussion of caring actions toward others. Encourage the children to participate. Show respect to the children and the ideas they present, so the children will feel comfortable about offering ideas in front of their classmates.

Write the caring actions the students mention on the chalkboard so that the children not only hear them but see them. Caring actions named might include the following:

assist parents with chores

share games and toys with friends

pray for those in need

make a get-well card for someone who is ill

contribute canned goods to a food pantry

help a neighbor

smile at someone who is feeling sad

give money to the missions

say hello to someone who is lonely

visit a nursing home

Ask the children to choose an activity to do during the coming week. Remind them that we are called to show care for others in Jesus' name and ask them to watch for opportunities to help others.

Heart Banner

Children can make individual felt banners as a reminder that God loves them and wants them to share that love with others. Pieces of red felt precut to 9" by 12" can be purchased inexpensively at fabric stores. Each piece makes the background for one banner. Have the children fold under the top inch and glue it along the edge to form a rod pocket. Regular school glue can be used. Notch the bottom edge of the banner with a scissors for a decorative effect.

Each child should cut out four letters from white felt to spell the word *love*. (Sharp scissors are needed to work with felt.) Help those children who have difficulty cutting. Have the children glue the letters diagonally down the banner from left to right. Then show each child how to cut out two white hearts and glue them to the banner for decoration.

Thread a wooden dowel through the pocket at the top of each banner. Then tie a length of red yarn to both ends of the dowel to form a hanger for the banner.

This project results in lovely heart banners to display at home as a reminder to love one another. The banners can also be given as a gift. Children enjoy working on craft projects and delight in having something to take home with them. These banners help children remember to share God's love with other people in their lives.

Our Neighbors

This prayer service helps the students learn to pray for God's help in caring about other people. It calls them to realize that God is always with us. It is important to recall that Jesus wants each of us to help others. This prayer service involves all the students in the class.

Who Is Our Neighbor?*

Leader:
> We gather together to celebrate our friendship in Christ.

Reader 1:
> This gospel reading is taken from Luke, chapter 10, verses 25 to 28. (*scripture reading*)

First group:
> Lord, help us to love God with our whole heart, our whole soul, and with all our strength.

Second group:
> Lord, help us to love our neighbors as ourselves.

Reader 2:
> To answer the question "Who is our neighbor?" Jesus told a story. This parable is taken from Luke, chapter 10, verses 29 to 37. (*scripture reading*)

First group:
> Lord, help us to love God with our whole heart, our whole soul, and with all our strength.

Second group:
> Lord, help us to love our neighbors as ourselves.

Reader 1:
> Which of the three proved to be a good neighbor to the man who was attacked by robbers?

Reader 2:
> The one who took pity on the man proved to be a good neighbor.

First group:
> Lord, help us to love God with our whole heart, our whole soul, and with all our strength.

Second group:
> Lord, help us to love our neighbors as ourselves.

Leader:
> Lord Jesus, we ask your help to become the people you want us to be.

Reader 1:
> When someone new moves into the neighborhood or there is a new student in the class ...

All:
> Lord, help us to become good friends and neighbors in your name.

Reader 2:
> When someone is lonely and needs friends ...

All:
> Lord, help us to become good friends and neighbors in your name.

Reader 1:
> When someone is treated unfairly or unkindly ...

All:
> Lord, help us to become good friends and neighbors in your name.

Reader 2:
> When someone needs help with something ...

All:
> Lord, help us to become good friends and neighbors in your name.

Reader 1:
> When someone is lied about or talked about in a mean way ...

All:
> Lord, help us to become good friends and neighbors in your name.

Reader 2:

When someone is hurt ...

All:

Lord, help us to become good friends and neighbors in your name.

Reader 1:

When someone is left out ...

All:

Lord, help us to become good friends and neighbors in your name.

Reader 2:

For all those who need our friendship ...

All:

Lord, help us to become good friends and neighbors in your name.

Leader:

Jesus, help us to always remember the story you told about the Good Samaritan. May we learn the lesson you taught and practice love of God and of neighbor in all that we do. These things we ask in your name.

All:

Amen.

Social Ministry Speaker

Many times students are unaware of the sad conditions under which some people live in their own community. It is important that students understand that some people are in desperate need, and that it is up to us as Christians to aid them in any way we can.

One way to help students become more aware of people in need is through a classroom speaker. Ask someone from a social ministry program in the parish, the diocese, or the community to speak to the children.

Ask the speaker to describe the needs in the local area and also some of the economic and social conditions that led to this need. Many times people can find themselves in serious circumstances through no fault of their own. It is also helpful if the speaker can give specific examples of people who have come to their attention. This helps students better understand the need. The speaker should also explain what his or her ministry does to aid these people both immediately and in the long term.

Follow the speaker's visit with class discussion. Talk about how each person is important — created in the image of God and loved by God. Remind the students that Jesus calls us to love others. If possible, ask the students to contribute to the social service agency in some way. Perhaps they could collect needed items, make a donation, or volunteer their time. Maybe their parents would be interested in helping as a family project.

Remind students that we need to pray for those who are in need. We should pray that God will help them work through their problems. We should also ask for God's help in finding a way for us to be of service. Remember the ministry of the speaker in the classroom prayers, and ask the students to pray at home for people in need.

Food Donations

Collecting items for a parish food pantry or local charity is a way of helping others. To encourage donations on a regular basis, highlight one needed item each month. Check with the organization that distributes the food to determine the most critical needs.

Place boxes in strategic locations to make it easy for people to give. Each month put a sign on the boxes with the food item being requested and glue sample labels on the boxes as well. This will remind people what is being collected that month. A sample calendar of food items follows:

August	*rice*
September	*canned fruit*
October	*macaroni and cheese*
November	*canned soup*
December	*peanut butter*
January	*dried milk*
February	*cereal*
March	*canned vegetables*
April	*boxed potatoes*
May	*canned stew*
June	*dried beans*
July	*baby food*

This method helps keep the students interested in donating food throughout the year, rather than just once. The decorated boxes remind people of the needs of others and help keep pantry shelves full.

Discussion Starters

Students can learn a great deal from listening to one another in the classroom. Sometimes students need to be reminded that they have many opportunities to show caring to other people. We are to see Jesus in one another.

Use the following scenarios as discussion starters for the students. Encourage the children to think of various ways in which they can help another person. There is no one correct way to respond to these situations. Help the students explore several different outcomes for each situation.

A girl in your school broke her leg. She is back in school today but is using crutches. You notice that she has been having difficulty carrying things and now it is lunch time. How can you help?

Some children at recess are teasing another child. They are calling him names and a group has surrounded him. What can you do?

The news accounts are full of stories about a hurricane. Many people have lost their homes and all their belongings. Is there anything that you can do to help them?

A friend in your neighborhood is moving to another state. She doesn't want to move. She has always lived in the same house. Now she has to move to a new house. She will be going to a new school too. What can you do for this friend?

A student in your class has cancer. He wears a baseball cap to school because the cancer treatment made his hair fall out. The other students avoid him because they don't know what to say. Is there anything you can say or do for him?

Your teacher looks sad today. He doesn't joke around with the class the way he usually does. How can you help?

A classmate was not chosen for a special project. She really wanted to be in the group of students that was selected. This is not the first time that this has happened to this girl. What can you say or do?

Your friend's parents are separating. He is really upset, but doesn't want to talk about it. You are afraid that he blames himself for what is happening in his family. Is there anything you can do for him?

Your grandma is sick. She lives with your family. Everyone is concerned about her, and that is all they talk about. Your grandma used to be fun to talk to, but now she forgets things. What should you do?

Your sister needs help with her math. You know how to do the problems, but you don't get along with her. She is always teasing you and going through your things. Should you offer to help her?

Students need guidance in exploring ways in which they can help others. When students have the opportunity to discuss various ways to be of service, they will be better able to see other situations in their lives that need a caring touch. Thinking about how they themselves would feel in a particular situation can lead to a greater awareness of the needs of other people.

Drawing

One way to help children think about how they can show caring toward others is through art. It is helpful to children when a discussion of loving others is followed by the opportunity to express their thoughts and ideas in a picture.

Encourage the children to draw themselves helping someone else. Provide paper and markers for them to use. Ask the students to label their papers "I Can Care." The act of drawing encourages children to think about caring in their own lives. They must relate what they have learned to life outside the classroom, and that is what religious education is all about.

Drawing activities also provide an opportunity for students who are not good at expressing their ideas with words. Through drawing, the students are able to articulate ideas that come from their hearts. Art work encourages creative thinking and allows for personal expression.

Ways of showing care for others are often best expressed visually. Pictures can speak to — and for — children. Young children enjoy sharing artwork with other students and explaining what they have drawn. This not only helps the children know that their ideas are valuable, but can be a source of learning for the other children in the class.

Coupon Booklet

Children need guidance in learning how to follow Jesus' command to love one another. They need to practice ways of helping others in their lives. One suitable activity for children is making "coupon booklets" to give away. Each booklet is filled with favors or chores that the child is willing to do for someone else.

Discuss with the children ideas for chores they would be willing to do, such as setting the table, raking leaves, taking out the trash, babysitting, or walking the dog. The choice of chores should be geared to the person they have in mind as the recipient. The final decision of which favors to include should be up to the individual child.

Each child will need about six pieces of paper for the booklet. (Each sheet of standard-size paper yields three pieces.) Each page of the booklet should be a different color. On each of five pieces of paper have the children print "This coupon good for ..." and list a chore they are willing to do. Then at the bottom of each page the children should sign their names. Borders or artwork enhance the look of each coupon. Use one page for the cover, on which the children print "Coupon Booklet." Assemble the pages and staple on the left side.

This activity helps students show care and love for someone else in their lives. It is a practical way to help a parent, grandparent, neighbor, or other recipient. The coupon booklet is a welcome gift of love.

Get-Well Letters

We must provide opportunities for children to show that they care. One way for them to do this is by writing get-well letters to a person in the hospital. A teacher, parent, or child will enjoy receiving letters from the children.

Explain to the children who recipient is and why he or she is in the hospital. Ask them to write a note to this person to cheer him or her. Encourage the children also to remember this person in their prayers. A get-well letter usually turns out like this:

> Dear Mrs. Smith,
>
> I am sorry you are in the hospital. I hope you get better soon. My class is remembering you in our prayers.
>
> Your friend,
> Amy

Encourage the children to illustrate the letter with drawings to make it bright and cheerful. Mail the letters together, or if possible deliver them in person to the hospital. Also pray for the person in class each time the children meet. These letters are a welcome and heartwarming gift for someone who is ill; it shows the person that he or she is thought about and remembered by the children. This is a great way to help students learn to help other people.

Teddy Bear Project

A terrific service project for children is to collect teddy bears. Many local police and fire departments like to keep teddy bears on hand to give to children in times of crisis. A cuddly teddy bear can be something to hold onto for a frightened child who is lost or hurt or the victim of a fire. This project enables children to help other children in a meaningful and useful way.

Send notes home describing this service project and enlisting parent support. The project is easy to explain, and support can be recruited quickly. Everyone understands that children in need can be comforted by a furry and lovable teddy bear.

Check with the local police and fire departments about their needs. They usually need many bears so that some are readily available in each police car and fire truck. Involve the whole church or school in this project in order to collect as many bears as possible.

Provide large collection boxes in the hallway or church vestibule clearly marked for the children's teddy bear project. Specify more than one collection date so that those who forget can bring their bears the next time they come to church or school. Empty the boxes between collection times, and keep the bears in a safe place until the delivery date.

The teddy bear project benefits children in crisis and helps other children learn to care.

Caring Poster

Visual images help us learn and remember. Students can create individual caring posters to enable them to understand ways that people can help one another.

Provide small posterboard sheets, about 11" by 14", for the students to use. Help them find appropriate pictures in family magazines, mission magazines, and discarded student texts. Each picture should depict a way of showing care for another person. Good pictures include:

Parents and children

Different nationalities working together

Literacy volunteer

Child helping another child

Elderly person helping someone younger

Missionary sharing the word of God

Someone helping a person with a handicap

Soup kitchen volunteer

Person collecting roadside litter

Nurse aiding someone who is injured

The different shapes and sizes of the pictures make interesting posters. Have the children arrange the pictures on the posterboard before gluing. The only word necessary on the posters is "Caring." Add it with self-stick letters or stencils.

When the posters are completed, ask the students to tell how each picture shows one person caring for another.

St. Vincent de Paul

The lives of the saints show us ways in which people have lived Jesus' command to love God and love others. St. Vincent de Paul dedicated his life to helping other people; he is called the Apostle of Charity.

St. Vincent de Paul was a French priest who lived in the 1600s. He tried to make life better for the poor people in Paris and especially for those who lived in the rural countryside. His followers served in hospitals, prisons, and orphanages. We celebrate the feast day of this saint on September 27. The St. Vincent de Paul Society, started by an admirer of this saint, continues today to minister to those in need.

Help students become familiar with the story of St. Vincent de Paul. They need to understand that this saint responded to the needs of the people he saw around him. We too must serve those in need in our communities. Encourage the students to discuss a class project that would benefit others. They could collect used winter clothing and donate it to the St. Vincent de Paul Society. Warm coats are especially needed by children in the winter time in cold climates. Ask the students to show concern for the poor as St. Vincent de Paul did. Help them to understand that Jesus calls us to share our time, our talents, our resources, and ourselves with others.

Service Project

It is important that students have opportunities to serve others in need. This helps them understand how they can help others and provides assistance to those who need it. A class service project helps students work together.

Check with local service agencies to determine what help is really needed; don't make assumptions. Money can be donated to an organization, but it is even better to collect items that are needed. One useful service project that benefits children is collecting baby articles for a day-care center that helps low-income families. These centers are set up so that a parent can work or go to school while the child is cared for a few hours a day.

These centers need items such as baby blankets, crib sheets, infant formula, bibs, disposable diapers, wipes, baby lotion, powder, trash bags, toys, baby food, small spoons, tissues, and the like. Supplies are used up very rapidly and need to be replenished often for the comfort and health of babies and young children.

Explain the project and the need to the class, and also send home a note asking the support of the parents. Children can readily understand the need for these items and are usually quite willing to contribute something. Participation should be entirely voluntary.

Helping the Homeless

God calls us to love others. We are to be compassionate as Jesus was compassionate. We are to see him in all people. We must reach out to help others. There are people in need even in our own communities.

One group that needs assistance is the homeless people who live on the street. These people find themselves in desperate circumstances. This is a complex issue with no easy answers, but we clearly are called to help in any way we can. Homeless shelters may offer such people their only opportunity to clean up and sleep in a warm place at night.

Individual toiletry items are usually in great demand at shelters. Soap, shampoo, toothpaste, toothbrushes, and razors are needed when shelters are filled to capacity night after night. Older students probably have seen news reports on television about the homeless problem. Ask them to coordinate a collection of supplies needed by a local shelter.

Publicity is important. Students can make posters to let others know of this project and give them the opportunity to help the homeless. Make announcements to classes and parishioners. Give out flyers. Provide marked boxes in appropriate locations for contributions.

If possible, take some of the students to the shelter when the items are delivered so they can see the need firsthand. Be sure to let the other students and parishioners know how much was collected and that their contributions are appreciated. This helps all who were involved to understand what we can do when we work together for the good of other people.

Global Awareness

We are responsible for what happens in our world. Students must learn that we are also called to assist people beyond our own immediate circumstances.

Discuss with the students different groups of people who may need help and ways students can be of assistance. Begin with groups familiar to the students and move toward awareness of our global responsibility.

Family:	assist with chores help a brother or sister
Friends:	cheer up a sad friend bring homework to a sick classmate
Neighbors:	visit a lonely neighbor pick up trash
Community:	contribute blankets to a homeless shelter visit a nursing home
Nation:	write a letter to an elected official use natural resources conservatively
World:	pray for those living in drought-stricken areas contribute to Catholic Relief Services sponsor a child in another country

Encourage thoughtful answers and ones that are creative. We need creative thinkers to help solve the problems of today and of the future. We may not be able to control what happens in the world, but we can choose how we will respond.

Praying for Others

As Christians we must be people who pray for the needs of others. We must acknowledge our dependence upon God in all things. Part of caring about people is praying for their needs. We can pray together as a community of God's people for the needs of those who are in difficult circumstances. In this way we are also reminded of the many conditions in our world that need change and improvement.

Use the following prayer in the classroom to pray for the needs of others:

> Our loving God, you are the source of life and of the hope of new life for all the peoples of the earth. You are like a loving father and mother to each.... Continue to open our hearts to all our sisters and brothers ... wherever they are ... however worthy or unworthy ... especially the poor and oppressed.... Inspire our creativity and deepen our generosity in working for a more just world order ... one that will serve the needs of all your people.... We ask this in the name of Jesus and in the power of his Spirit. Amen.*

We must as a church community be dedicated to helping others as Jesus taught us. We must be concerned for the victims of poverty, war, discrimination, and all those in need of assistance. We must be committed to them and ready to live out our concern by our actions. We are responsible for making our faith a reality in the world.

Works of Mercy

Our commitment to those in need is clearly spelled out by Jesus:

> For I was hungry and you gave me food, I was thirsty and you gave me drink, a stranger and you welcomed me, naked and you clothed me, ill and you cared for me.... Whatever you did for one of these least brothers of mine, you did for me (Mt 25:35–40).

Discuss this Bible reading with the students. What is our responsibility to those who are hungry in our communities? What about the children who are starving in other countries? Is there a solution to the problem of those who are homeless and living on the street? What about those who live in refugee camps in war-torn nations? What can we do about those who live in poverty? How should we treat those who are in some way different from us?

It is important for the students to realize that it is our responsibility, both as individuals and as a society, to see that people have what they need to live. Each of us is given life by God and created in God's image. Each human life is sacred. We have an obligation to safeguard the rights and dignity of other people. We will be judged by God by how we care about the needs of others.

There are no easy answers to the problems in our world. But each of us must strive to live the gospel values in our lives. As teachers we must help students become aware of our responsibility to all people. We must work together to show care and concern for others. We must see the face of Jesus in these people, just as Jesus himself reminds us in this reading from Matthew.

Chapter 3

We Are Called to
Live the Word of God

The Bible tells the story of God and of God's people. The central event of the Bible is the life, death, and resurrection of Jesus Christ. This is the most important event in the history of humankind. Through Jesus we have new life with God.

The Hebrew scriptures tell the story of the chosen people. The forty-six books record how the Israelites kept faith in one God alive through the centuries. The Christian scriptures tell how God fulfilled his promise to the chosen people by sending his Son. The twenty-seven books show what Jesus' coming meant for the people of God and also records the founding of the church.

Through the Bible we are called to a life with God. The Bible is the word of God speaking to us in our lives. God's message is found in the people and events of scripture. Jesus showed us how we can live by his life and through the stories he told. Through the Bible God calls us to follow his Son and to live his word in our lives.

God reveals himself to us through the Bible, which records the relationship of the people to their God. The books of the Bible show God's unending love for us.

The Bible developed under the guidance and inspiration of the Holy Spirit. God used human authors and human stories to speak to human people. The books of the Bible were written by many different people for many different groups over a span of centuries.

No new books have been added to the Bible since the second century when the leaders of the church at that time decided what would be included in the official scriptures of the church. The church remains the final authority in interpreting the Bible. History, literature, and tradition are carefully taken into account in interpreting the message of scripture for our times.

Through the Bible God continues to call us to be faithful. We are to respond to that call and live God's word in our lives. Each generation must hear anew the stories of scripture that tell us who we are. It is very important to help children know and understand the message of the Bible and the scripture stories that speak to our hearts. We must help them hear God's call in their lives.

Bible Verses

Students need practice looking up specific verses so they will become more familiar with the words of the Bible. Ask the students to find Bible verses, such as the following. They should write down the words next to the reference. (The words are given in parentheses here for the convenience of the teacher.) All students should use the same Bible translation to avoid confusion.

HEBREW SCRIPTURES/ OLD TESTAMENT

Psalm 25:4 — (Your ways, O LORD, make known to me; teach me your paths)

Leviticus 26:12 — (Ever present in your midst, I will be your God, and you will be my people)

Isaiah 55:6 — (Seek the LORD while he may be found, call him while he is near)

CHRISTIAN SCRIPTURES/ NEW TESTAMENT

Mark 12:30 — (You shall love the Lord your God with all your heart, with all your soul, with all your mind, and with all your strength)

John 8:12 — (Jesus spoke to them again, saying, "I am the light of the world. Whoever follows me will not walk in darkness, but will have the light of life")

Romans 15:13 — (May the God of hope fill you with all joy and peace in believing so that you may abound in hope by the power of the Holy Spirit)

If the students are new at this, it is a good idea to work with the class as a whole before beginning individual work. Point out the pages in the Bible where the books are listed and page numbers given. Ask the students to find selected books in the Bible and tell on what page the book starts and ends.

For younger children the teacher may want to put markers at the beginning of each book from which the above verses are taken. That way students will get started in the right part of the Bible.

While students are looking up the verses, walk around the room and help the students who need it. Comment positively on the progress of all the students. When they have finished, ask for volunteers to read the verses that go with each reference.

Tissue Rainbow

The rainbow reminds us that God always keeps his promises. In Genesis 9 the rainbow is a sign of God's covenant with Noah and his promise to all generations. God will be faithful to Noah, who was faithful to God.

A colorful craft that helps remind the students of God's faithfulness is a tissue rainbow.* Students can draw a rainbow or the teacher can duplicate the pattern for each student on blue paper. Inside the arch of the rainbow each student should print "God keeps promises." Have the students attach the paper to the same size posterboard with a glue stick so that the project will be sturdy.

Supply the students with different colors of tissue paper. Have them cut the paper into 1 1/2" squares. Each student should choose three colors for the rainbow, such as red, yellow, and blue. Then the student covers one band of the rainbow with glue, takes one of the tissue squares and wraps it around the eraser end of a pencil, and presses it onto the rainbow. It will stick to the glue. Continue with one color until the entire band is covered with paper squares.

Then the student puts glue on the next band and repeats the process with another color of tissue squares. Finally, each student completes his or her rainbow with a third color. Have the students punch two holes in the top and use a length of yarn to hang up the finished craft.

The tissue rainbow is a simple craft that produces beautiful and colorful rainbows for the children. Each one is a little different. This project is a good way to remind students that God keeps his promises.

Name Bingo

An interesting way to help students review names of people from the Hebrew scriptures is to play bingo. Draw a grid on paper with sixteen squares of equal size. In each square print or type one name, such as:

Abraham	Isaiah
Moses	Deborah
Ruth	Samuel
Miriam	Joshua
Esther	Joseph
Jacob	David
Judith	Solomon
Elijah	Sarah

Other names of figures the students have been studying can also be used. Make additional bingo cards using various arrangements of the names so that each card is different. Cut one of the cards into squares and put the squares into a box.

To play the game give each student a bingo card. Also provide unpopped popcorn or small pieces of colored paper to use as markers. Choose one name from the box and call it out. The students mark that name on their card. Play continues until one student has marked four squares in a row, either across, down, or diagonally across the card. More than one student may have bingo at the same time. Give each winner a prize, perhaps a Bible verse pencil or bookmark. Then clear the cards and begin the game again.

This is a good activity for review. It really involves the students and makes learning a challenging experience. Name bingo also allows all members of the class to participate in a group activity.

Psalm Pictures

The words of the psalms can help students express praise, thanksgiving, and petition to God. Students can illustrate some beautiful verses from the psalms by using pictures cut from magazines and travel booklets. The following are good verses to use:

O LORD, our Lord,
　　how glorious is your name over all
　　　　the earth! (Psalm 8:10).

Therefore will I proclaim you, O LORD,
　　among the nations,
and I will sing praise to your name (Psalm 18:50).

All the ends of the earth
　　shall remember and turn to the LORD (Psalm 22:28).

To you I lift up my soul,
　　O LORD, my God.
In you I trust (Psalm 25:1).

Hear, O God, my cry;
　　listen to my prayer! (Psalm 61:2).

We give you thanks, O God, we give
　　thanks,
　　and we invoke your name; we
　　　　declare your wondrous deeds (Psalm 75:2).

From the rising to the setting of the
　　sun
is the name of the LORD to be
　　praised (Psalm 113:3).

My help is from the LORD,
　　who made heaven and earth (Psalm 121:2).

Let everything that has breath
　　praise the LORD! Alleluia (Psalm 150:6).

Each student can choose a different psalm verse and an appropriate picture to illustrate it. Suggest cutting the picture in an irregular shape to add interest. Then have the students glue their pictures onto sheets of construction paper and print the words of the psalm verse under the picture. This psalm artwork is a colorful addition to any hallway and helps the students understand the feelings and images expressed in the psalms. Such a display is a source of inspiration and reflection to all who pass by it.

O Lord, our Lord
how glorious is your
name over all the
earth. Psalm 8:10

Psalm 23

The image of the good shepherd is found in both parts of the Bible. In Psalm 23 God is compared to a shepherd who watches over the sheep.

Psalm 23 can be adapted as a prayer led by the teacher. After each phrase the students respond, "The Lord is my shepherd." Such an adaptation of the psalm follows:

Teacher: The Lord is my shepherd: I shall not want.
   Children: **The Lord is my shepherd.**

Teacher: In green pastures he gives me rest.
   Children: **The Lord is my shepherd.**

Teacher: Beside the water he leads me and refreshes me.
   Children: **The Lord is my shepherd.**

Teacher: He guides me in the right path.
   Children: **The Lord is my shepherd.**

Teacher: Even in the darkness I am not afraid.
   Children: **The Lord is my shepherd.**

Teacher: For the Lord will defend me and give me courage.
   Children: **The Lord is my shepherd.**

Teacher: And I will dwell in the house of the Lord.
   Children: **The Lord is my shepherd.**

This reassuring image of God helps the students to know that God is always with us and always cares for us.

Good News

The following echo pantomime describes the beginning of Jesus' public ministry. By repeating the words and actions line by line after the teacher, students can tell the story. This pantomime is based on Matthew 4:23–25, which tells of Jesus ministering to the multitude who followed him.

Jesus went around Galilee	*(walk in place)*
teaching in the synagogues.	*(hands by mouth)*
He proclaimed the gospel	*(arms outstretched)*
and cured every illness.	*(hand on forehead)*
Sick people were brought to him	*(arms on chest)*
and he made them well.	*(right arm forward)*
And great crowds of people	*(swing hand left to right)*
followed him everywhere.	*(walk in place)*
Jesus taught the good news	*(hands by mouth)*
about God's love.	*(hug self)*

An echo pantomime involves the students in the Bible lesson and helps them remember the story — and what it means. Echo pantomimes are a favorite activity of many students, an activity they enjoy doing time after time.

Jesus Litany

There are many images of Jesus in the gospels. Help the students compose a Jesus litany to use as a class prayer. Invite students to contribute ideas, which are written on the chalkboard. Then each phrase of the litany can be followed by "Hear our prayer." A Jesus litany might be like this:

> Jesus, Bread of Life,
>   hear our prayer.
> Jesus, Good Shepherd,
>   hear our prayer.
> Jesus, forgiver of sins,
>   hear our prayer.
> Jesus, Savior and Messiah,
>   hear our prayer.
> Jesus, Word of God,
>   hear our prayer.
> Jesus, compassionate healer,
>   hear our prayer.
> Jesus, light of the world.
>   hear our prayer.

This type of prayer offers insight to many students because of the varied images of Jesus it reflects. This prayer can be used as a follow-up to a lesson on the gospels or the life of Jesus. It helps draw together various images of Jesus for the students.

Echo Pantomime

The story of the loaves and fishes is especially appropriate for an echo pantomime. The teacher says a line and does the motions. The children echo the words and actions line by line.

A great crowd followed Jesus	*(open arms wide)*
as he walked up the mountain.	*(walk in place)*
The people were hungry	*(rub stomach)*
for they had come a long way.	*(walk in place)*
There was not enough food	*(shake head no)*
for five thousand people to eat.	*(bring hand to mouth)*
But a boy in the crowd	*(hand parallel to ground)*
had five loaves and two fish.	*(hold up five fingers)*
Jesus told the people	*(hold arms in front)*
to sit on the grass.	*(point to ground)*
Jesus took the loaves and fish	*(hold palms upturned)*
and thanked God for the food.	*(bow head and fold hands)*
Jesus gave food to the people	*(hold palms upturned)*
and they ate and ate.	*(bring hand to mouth)*
The disciples gathered leftovers	*(gathering motions)*
and there were twelve baskets full.	*(make arms round)*
Jesus shared with people	*(hold arms in front)*
and they shared with one another.	*(nod head)*

This way of telling a Bible story helps children understand it. They almost feel as if they had been there. An echo pantomime story enables the students to remember a story longer, because they were actively involved in the telling. This is an excellent way to work with children and Bible stories.

Computer Banner

An eye-catching banner can be made on a computer. A parent, teacher, or student is usually willing to print out on a home computer a banner bearing the words of a Bible verse. This banner is simple to do with a computer that has a banner program. The banner is printed on a long continuous sheet of paper, and the letters are large and easy to read.

Bible verses that can be used for a banner include the following:

Let the children come to me (Mark 10:14).

I am with you always (Matthew 28:20).

Love one another (John 15:7).

Rejoice in the Lord always (Philippians 4:4).

I am the resurrection and the life (John 11:25).

Have the students use markers to color in or outline the letters spelling out the Bible verse. Then they can cut pictures from magazines to add colorful illustrations to the banner. The choice of pictures will depend on the message of the Bible verse. Attach the pictures with a glue stick.

Hang the banner in the hallway with push pins for all to see. Cork tacking strips along the wall are ideal for hanging banners and other art work throughout the year.

Lost Sheep Game

Young children can learn about God's love for them through carefully selected gospel stories. The story of the lost sheep in Matthew 18:12–14 says to children that God cares about each of them.

A great activity that goes along with this Bible story is the lost sheep game. This game helps children understand the story and engages their interest. All the children in the class play together. The children play the game while singing the words to the tune of "London Bridge Is Falling Down."

One Little Sheep Is Lost*

Part 1

Two children stand with arms together to make a bridge. Other children pass under and sing. The arms come down "catching" the one sheep on the last line.

Verse 1

All the sheep come home at night, home at night, home at night. All the sheep come home at night. All but one!

Part 2

The two children with the caught sheep sway back and forth to the music. The other children hold hands and form a circle around the three.

Verse 2

Let's go find the little sheep, little sheep, little sheep. Let's go find the little sheep. Because God loves him (her).

Part 3

The outer circle comes in to the three children and takes them back out so that all are in one circle.

Verse 3

Now we've found our little sheep, little sheep, little sheep. Now we've found our little sheep. Let's take him (her) home again.

Part 4

Children skip in a circle holding hands. Quickly choose two more children to make a bridge and begin again.

Verse 4

Now we'll have a party, a party, a party. Now we'll have a party. Our little sheep is found.

Children like to play games that involve singing and action. This game helps children to be active participants in the class. They remember the story and understand it better when they have been involved.

Lame Man Story

An echo pantomime involves the children in telling a Bible story. Children echo the teacher's words and actions line by line. An echo pantomime for the story of the lame man in Luke 5:17–26 follows:

One day Jesus was teaching	*(hands cup mouth)*
and many people came to hear.	*(hand cups ear)*
Two people carried a stretcher	*(hold up two fingers)*
with a man who couldn't walk.	*(touch leg)*
But the crowd was so large	*(stretch out arms)*
they couldn't get through.	*(pushing motions)*
So they lowered the man	*(push down)*
through the roof to Jesus.	*(nod head)*
Jesus said to the man,	*(hands cup mouth)*
"Your sins are forgiven."	*(hold out arm)*
People said to one another,	*(open and close hand)*
"How can he forgive sins	*(shrug shoulders)*
when only God can do that?"	*(point up)*
Jesus knew what they were thinking	*(point to head)*
and said to the lame man,	*(hands cup mouth)*
"Rise and walk."	*(push hands up)*
The lame man stood up	*(straighten shoulders)*
and walked away praising God.	*(walk in place)*
The people were amazed	*(hands palms up)*
at what they had seen.	*(point to eyes)*

An echo pantomime Bible story such as this one is meaningful to the children. The motions and words help them understand the story. Echo pantomime stories hold the attention and interest of the children.

Jesus and Zacchaeus Playlet

The following playlet helps children understand the story of Jesus and Zacchaeus. Reading the parts helps them see what is going on in this important Bible story about forgiveness.

The reader can be a student or the teacher. Students should read the parts of Zacchaeus and Jesus.* Other students can be the crowd.

Reader:	One day Jesus was passing through the town of Jericho. A very rich tax collector named Zacchaeus lived there. He was eager to see Jesus.
Zacchaeus:	Jesus is in town. How great! I always did want to see him.
Reader:	But the crowd was so large, and Zacchaeus was so short, that he couldn't see anything.
Zacchaeus:	(*Disappointed*) Oh, I can't see a thing. (*Suddenly cheering up*) I know what I can do. I'll climb this sycamore tree so that when Jesus passes by, I'll get to see him.
Reader:	So he ran ahead and climbed the sycamore tree to get a glimpse of Jesus. When Jesus reached the spot he looked right up into the tree and said,
Jesus:	Zacchaeus, come down. Hurry, I must stay at your house today.
Reader:	Zacchaeus could hardly believe it.
Zacchaeus:	Who, me, Lord?
Reader:	Then Zacchaeus hurried down and welcomed Jesus with great joy.
Zacchaeus:	Welcome, welcome to my house, Jesus. I am so happy to have you come!
Reader:	When they saw what was happening, some of the people in the crowd started complaining.
Crowd:	Jesus has gone to stay at the house of a sinner!

Reader: But something happened at Zacchaeus' house. Zacchaeus felt sorry that he had cheated people when he collected their tax money. He stood up and said to the Lord,

Zacchaeus: Look, Sir. I am going to give half of all I own to the poor. If I have cheated anybody, I will pay back four times the amount.

Jesus: The blessing of God has come to this house today.

Good Shepherd Banner

One way to help children understand that Jesus cares about each of us is to share the story of the Good Shepherd found in John 10:11–17. Discuss the image in this story with the students. Then work with them to create a Good Shepherd banner.

Make this banner out of felt, which can be purchased by the yard at fabric stores. Green is an appropriate background color for this banner because it is the color of the grass where sheep graze. Depending on the height of the banner stand the class will use, purchase about 6' of felt. The width of the banner will be the width of the bolt of felt (3'). Hem the top and bottom 3" to form rod pockets. Insert inexpensive round drapery rods so the banner hangs straight. Then tie a length of cord to the ends of the top drapery rod in order to hang the banner.

In the middle of the banner glue a long staff cut from gold felt to symbolize Jesus as the Good Shepherd. Explain the symbolism to the children. (The teacher can pin the staff to the banner instead; then the background can be used again.)

Duplicate a white paper sheep for each student. Ask the students to cut out the sheep and print their name in the center with a marker. Then have the children come forward one at a time to put their sheep on the banner as a sign that Jesus the Good Shepherd loves and cares for them. The sheep can be attached with straight pins or velcro.

This banner makes an effective part of a prayer service with background music playing on a song tape as the children come forward.

The Good Shepherd banner is a great way to personalize the Bible for children so that they can understand the message of God's love that is found there.

Chapter 4

We Are Called to Rejoice in Creation

Through the beauty of the world around us we can see God's presence in our lives. Our world is filled with wonderful gifts that God has made for love of us. The story of creation helps us to see God at work in our lives and to know that everything God made is good. We are called to rejoice in creation and all that God has done for us.

The lesson of creation is one that is learned for a lifetime. No matter what our age, the budding beauty of springtime reminds us that God cares for us. The majesty of a stately tree, the caress of a gentle breeze, the brilliant colors of blooming flowers, and the kindness of other people are all reminders of God's presence and love. Every time we admire a golden sunset or hear a child laugh we know that God is with us.

Children are fascinated by the vastness and variety of creation. We can use the wonders of creation to help children understand that God is at work in our world as Father and Creator. God is the source of all that is good. We must help the children respond to God's creation with praise and thanksgiving. We must help them celebrate creation and God's love for us.

Picture Story

The biblical story of how God created the world can be told to children using pictures taken from travel booklets, garden catalogs, and nature magazines.

Mount appropriate pictures on colored posterboard. (Cut the posterboard larger than the picture to form a frame.) Cover the picture and posterboard with clear self-adhesive covering to make them durable.

Print the part of the story that goes with each picture on the back for the convenience of the teacher. As the pictures are shown to the children, the teacher reads the story from the backs of the pictures. The story and pictures to use follow:

Picture 1 — sunset

In the beginning there was nothing but darkness. Then God said, "Let there be light." And God made the sun to shine in the daytime and the stars to shine at night. And God saw that it was good.

Picture 2 — mountain and sky

Then God said, "Let there be dry land all around and the sky above." And God made the earth, and the mountains, and the blue sky. And God saw that it was good.

Picture 3 — flowers

Then God said, "Let there be trees and plants of every kind." And God made apple trees and oak trees. And God made red flowers and yellow flowers. And God saw that it was good.

Picture 4 — birds and/or fish

Then God said, "Let there be birds to fly in the sky and fish to swim in the sea." And there were robins and doves and fish of every color. And God saw that it was good.

Picture 5 — animals

Then God said, "Let there be animals of all kinds." And God made elephants and giraffes and rabbits and kittens. And God saw that it was good.

Picture 6 — people

Then God said, "Let there be people." And God made people in God's own image. God made people to love God and love others — people who would laugh and cry and be happy. And God saw that everything was good.

This is the story of how God made our world.

This visual way of telling the story found in Genesis appeals to the children and is easy to do. The pictures keep the attention of the children focused on the story. It helps them understand that God made the world and that everything God made is good.

Sponge Print Butterfly

Children can make a multicolored butterfly as a reminder of the beautiful world God has made for us. Ask the children to cut out large butterfly shapes from manila paper. (The teacher can draw the shape on the paper to make this part easier.)

Then the children can decorate their butterflies with sponge painting. Cut household sponges into 1" squares. Attach clothespins as handles to keep fingers out of the paint. Put bright colors of tempera paint in individual containers. The children dip the sponge into the paint color of their choice and then press it lightly onto their butterflies.

For best results each color of paint should have its own sponge squares. Encourage the children to use colors they like and decorate the butterfly in any pattern they choose.

Art projects are fun and exciting for children and encourage God-given creativity. Children enjoy working on art activities in a group with other children.

The children can take home their butterflies and display them as a reminder of the beauty of God's creation. Each time they look at the butterfly they will remember the fun they had making it and think of the wonders of our world. Art work helps extend learning from the classroom to the home.

Cinquain Poem

Children enjoy composing their own poems about God's creation using an adaptation of the cinquain poetry form. Students and teacher can work together writing a class cinquain on the chalkboard.

The cinquain is a five-line poem. The form is as follows:

Title (one word)
Descriptive words (two words)
Action words (three words)
Phrase (four words)
Summary (one word)

A creation cinquain beginning with the word Creation could turn out like this:

Creation
Always changing
Growing, renewing, delighting
God made it all
Wonderful

In order to write a poem reflection like this, the students have to think about what creation means to them. After helping to write a class cinquain, the students can compose individual poems. Some students like to write about an individual part of creation, such as clouds, animals, flowers, sunshine, or people. The creation cinquain helps students express their feelings and ideas about creation.

Creation Booklet

Projects that can be taken home after class are exciting for the children to do. Making a booklet about God's wonderful world is a good idea for teaching about creation.

The inside pages of the booklet feature illustrations by the children with crayons or markers. The children should print the following captions at the bottom of each page and then draw an appropriate picture:

Page 1 *God made the sun*

Page 2 *God made the flowers*

Page 3 *God made the trees*

Page 4 *God made the animals*

Page 5 *God made the people*

Have the children assemble the completed pages in order. Title the front cover of the booklet "God's Wonderful World." Add the author's name. Colored paper is effective for the front and back cover. Staple the pages together or punch holes and insert brads.

Each booklet is a unique creation. Suggest that the children take home their creation booklets and read them to their families. These booklets serve to remind the children that God made our beautiful world.

Night-time Door Hanger

A door hanger is a good project for children. It can be displayed at home as a reminder that God made the stars we see in the night sky.

Use a half sheet of blue construction paper to represent the sky. Show the children how to round off the top edge of their paper and cut a hole near the top to slide over a doorknob. Duplicate the following verse for each child before class:

> Thank you, God,
>   for stars so bright
> That shine on me
>   in the night.
> Thank you, God,
>   for stars above
> That you made
>   for me with love!

Help the children glue the verse onto their door hangers. Then have them draw a decorative line around the outside edge and the doorknob hole. For the final touch, put self-stick stars in different colors on the hanger.

This project helps the children realize that God made all of our world. The hanger can be hung on the doorknob of their bedroom door to remind them that God is always with us, even at night and even in the dark.

Show and Tell

Announce a show-and-tell time to help the children become familiar with things that God has made. Ask the children to bring a nature item to the next class. Send home a note so that parents can help the children look for a suitable object. Items that are good for show and tell include the following:

bird nest	feather
flower	tree branch
stone	hamster
goldfish	leaf
plant	pine cone
apple	shell

Many interesting nature objects are brought in, and children get a close-up look at some of the things that God has made.

Ask the children to come forward one at a time and show the class what they have brought. Let them explain what it is, where they found it, and what they know about it. Then let other children ask questions if they wish.

This idea brings God's creation into the classroom in a way that the children can understand.

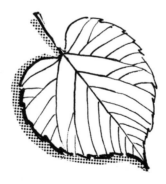

Window Garden

A good way to help children understand God's gift of creation is planting seeds. As the seeds sprout the children see the miracle of creation for themselves.

Make a window garden by using empty egg cartons. Cut the bottom of the cartons in half, so each child will have a planter with six compartments. Let the children fill each section with potting soil. (Be sure to put down newspaper first.)

Provide a variety of fast-growing seeds and ask the children to plant a few in each section. Explain that all living things, such as plants, need water and sunlight to grow. Let the children water their seeds with a spoon. Caution them against too much water. Then have children take home their gardens and place them on a sunny windowsill. In a week or so tiny green plants will sprout from the seeds, and the children will have their own miniature gardens.

Children enjoy tending their plants and watching them grow taller. This is a good activity for children who are learning about the wonders of God's creation because they have an active role.

Creation Acrostic

Learning to thank God for creation is important for children. One way to help them do this is to compose an acrostic creation prayer. In an acrostic each letter in the theme word is used as the beginning letter of another word. Ask the children to name something God made that begins with each letter in the word *creation*. Do this on a chalkboard or a piece of posterboard. Then use the acrostic as the center of a prayer.

Here is a sample creation acrostic prayer:

Dear God,
We thank you for the
world you have made
for love of us.
Thank you for

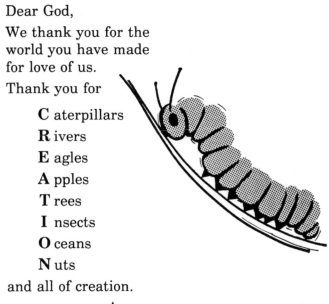

C aterpillars
R ivers
E agles
A pples
T rees
I nsects
O ceans
N uts

and all of creation.

Amen.

Children are interested in a prayer they helped to write, and they are able to understand a simple prayer such as this. A creation acrostic helps the children remember to thank God for the many gifts of creation.

Flower Banner

The variety and colors of flowers are truly amazing. Flowers are a lovely part of God's creation. They may not last, but the children can make fabric flower banners that do. They can take these individual banners home as a reminder of the wonder of our world and everything in it that God has made.

Each child needs a 10" by 15" piece of beige burlap. (Burlap is sold by the yard in fabric stores.) Cut the burlap before class, and sew a 1" hem at one end of each banner. This forms a place to insert the 12" wooden dowel from which the banner hangs.

To make the flowers children will need three colors of print fabric. Use an additional color to make the flowerpot. Have each child cut out three flower shapes and three small circles for flower centers as well as a flowerpot shape. (Provide patterns for the children to use for these shapes.) Sharp scissors make this process much easier. Provide green rickrack for stems for the flowers. Each child should cut one piece for each flower.

When all the cutting has been completed, ask the students to arrange all the pieces on the burlap. Then glue the pieces into place. Place paper under the burlap to catch any glue that comes through.

Tie a 15" piece of green yarn to both ends of the wooden dowel for a hanger. These bright, colorful banners look terrific; the students will be proud of them.

A flower banner is a student creation. It will help the children remember that everything in our world is a gift of God's love. These banners also make great gifts.

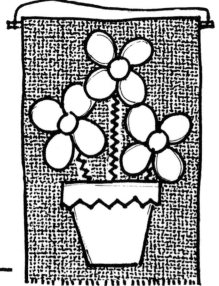

Guessing Game

A guessing game about creation helps children understand that God made the world they see around them. It helps them realize the great diversity of God's creation.

Ask the questions that follow one at a time and let the children call out the answer:

I'm thinking of something God made that waters all the plants and flowers. What is it? *(rain)*

I'm thinking of something God made that shines in the sky at night. What is it? *(star)*

I'm thinking of something God made that is colorful, has leaves, and smells good. What is it? *(flower)*

I'm thinking of something God made that grows on trees and is red and shiny. What is it? *(apple)*

I'm thinking of something God made that you see when you look up. It is blue and has clouds in it. What is it? *(sky)*

I'm thinking of something that God made that you can climb on, but it's a long way to the top. What is it? *(mountain)*

I'm thinking of something God made that can think, and laugh, and sing. What is it? *(person)*

Children can also take turns thinking of their own questions and asking the class to guess the answer. This type of activity helps the children learn by challenging them to think.

Creation Litany

God loves us so much that he made a beautiful world for us to enjoy. Our response to God should be one of praise and thanksgiving. We must help the children to express their gratitude to God. One way to do this is with a creation litany. Ask for six student volunteers to read parts of the prayer. All the rest of the children respond with the refrain.

Reader 1: For the beauty of the morning sun,
Children: We thank you, God, Father and Creator.

Reader 2: For flowers that bloom in a rainbow of colors,
Children: We thank you, God, Father and Creator.

Reader 3: For birds and fish and all the animals,
Children: We thank you, God, Father and Creator.

Reader 4: For the lakes and rivers and oceans,
Children: We thank you, God, Father and Creator.

Reader 5: For the stars in the sky and the vastness of space,
Children: We thank you, God, Father and Creator.

Reader 6: For all people created in your image and likeness,
Children: We thank you, God, Father and Creator.

A litany helps children put their ideas and feelings into words. It enables them to praise God in a way they can understand. A creation litany helps all of us remember the beauty of our world and its Creator.

Children's Rhyme

Young children enjoy learning activities in which they are active participants. The following action rhyme with motions for the children to do is fun and helps them explore the idea of God as a loving Creator:

God made the sun and the bright day time.
(fingers form a circle)

God made the night and the stars that shine.
(point upward)

God made the animals big and small.
(hold hand up, then down)

God made animals that hop and crawl.
(hop in place)

God made kittens who cuddle and purr.
(hands like paws, purr)

God made rabbits with soft white fur.
(pretend to stroke fur)

God made lions who can growl and roar.
(hands by mouth, roar)

God made birds and eagles that soar.
(arms outstretched like flying)

God made flowers that reach for the sun.
(stretch arms overhead)

God made children who play and run.
(run in place)

God made everything that we can see.
(arms open wide)

God made you and God made me.
(point to another and then self)

This action rhyme explains creation to children in a way that they can understand and uses images they know.

Sticker Story

Stickers can be used by children to illustrate the story of creation. Print the creation story on a sheet of typing paper and duplicate a copy for each child. You can use the following story, based on Genesis 1:1–31:

> God made the sun,
>   the moon, and stars.
> God made the trees,
>   the flowers and plants.
> God made the lions, bears,
>   and all the animals.
> Best of everything,
>   God made people!

Read the story to the children, and then have them add stickers to illustrate each sentence. (Change the words to fit the available stickers, if necessary.) Have the children glue the sticker story onto a colorful sheet of construction paper to provide a frame for the story.

The stickers help even nonreaders remember the creation story and the things God has made. The children can tell their families the story of creation by either reading the words or telling the story from the stickers. This idea helps the creation story from the Bible come alive for children.

Nature Bulletin Board

Nature pictures displayed on a hall bulletin board can remind children of the wonders that God has made. In the center of the bulletin board put letters cut from construction paper that say "God made our world."

Choose suitable nature pictures and carefully cut them out. Colorful pictures of flowers are found in garden catalogs, available free from mail-order nurseries. Pictures of children and families are common in ads in magazines. Beautiful pictures of mountains, rivers, and trees are plentiful in publications put out by state tourism bureaus. Appealing animal pictures are available in children's nature magazines.

Use a glue stick to attach the pictures to pieces of brightly colored construction paper. Pin the pictures in a pleasing arrangement around the words on the bulletin board. Six pictures are usually enough to illustrate our beautiful world.

Each time students pass by the bulletin board they will be reminded again of the scenic and wonderful world God has made for love of us.

Prayer of Praise

All of us need to pause and remember that everything we have is a gift from God. God made our world out of love for us, a love freely given that never ends.

The following creation prayer can help children express thanksgiving to God for all creation:

> Dear God, Creator of our world
>   and everything in it,
> We thank you for
>   the twinkle of stars at night
>   the vastness of the ocean
>   the majesty of the mountains
>   the softness of a puppy
>   the warmth of a summer breeze
>   the gift of friendship
>   the sound of voices raised in song
>   the care people show one another.
> Hear our prayer of praise. Everything
>   you have made is good.
>
> Amen.

This type of prayer reminds the children of the many gifts that God has given us in our lives. Prayers of thanksgiving are an important way of praising and honoring God as Creator of our universe and all its wonders.

Chapter 5

We Are Called to Pray Together

Prayer is our response to God's love and presence in our lives. As people of God we are called to pray together as a community. Prayer celebrates God's love for us and our relationship with him — Father, Son, and Holy Spirit.

Through prayer we express our faith in and love for God. Prayer should be part of who we are as Christians. It is important and must be woven into the fabric of our lives as a community. Prayer helps us open our minds and hearts to God. We are to pray for our own individual needs and the needs of others. Together we offer our prayers and petitions to God.

God speaks to us also in our lives during times of prayer and calls us to be faithful followers of his Son, Jesus Christ. Alive in the Spirit and united in the love of God, we pray as a community to God, who is the Father of us all, and who hears our prayers.

Prayer is a multidimensional experience; it takes many different forms. We pray at different times of the day, in different places, and in different circumstances of our lives. Prayer is also different things to different people. A variety of different prayer forms offers us different perspectives from which to see and hear and experience God.

One of our main tasks as religious educators is to help students build a relationship with God. Prayer is an important part of that relationship and holds it together. Prayer helps us explore our relationship with God and with one another. Prayer helps us to know God and to know ourselves. The only way to learn to pray is to do it. The more we pray together with the students, the more they will be able to make prayer a part of their lives. We are called to be people who pray, and we must help students experience many different forms of prayer. Opportunities for prayer in the classroom are essential.

Traditional Prayers

Traditional prayers are an important part of our Catholic heritage. They should be memorized and said communally as well as individually. Traditional prayers are an important way to pray. These prayers help us to express what we believe about God and ourselves.

We often say we have learned these prayers "by heart." This is a reminder of where these prayers must come from. Traditional prayers help us acknowledge our dependence on God and ask for God's assistance. These prayers help us praise God and celebrate the presence of God in our lives. They can be used to express sorrow for what we have done wrong. They help us to pray when we feel unable to pray. They help us — as they have Christians for hundreds of years — find comfort in times of sorrow and strength in times of distress. Such prayers are learned for a lifetime.

Some traditional prayers for the students to learn include the following:

Sign of the Cross	Act of Faith
Our Father	Act of Hope
Hail Mary	Act of Love
Glory Be	Morning offering
Act of Sorrow	Come Holy Spirit
Apostles Creed	Prayer of St. Francis
Mealtime grace	Divine Praises

These and other traditional prayers help students speak to God from the depths of their hearts. They help all of us direct our thoughts and words to God and to reflect on our relationship with God.

Spontaneous Prayer

Prayer should be a natural part of who we are as followers of Jesus. Spontaneous prayer is prayer that comes from our hearts in response to what is happening in our lives and the lives of others.

We need to model prayer for the children in our classes. It is important that they see the teacher as a person of prayer. The children should feel comfortable in bringing their prayer needs to the classroom.

Spontaneous prayer can take many forms. It can be a prayer of thanksgiving for a sunny day after a stormy night. It can be a prayer for others when a fire siren is heard outside. It can be a short remembrance of an ill relative included with the class prayer. It can be a moment of silent prayer for victims of a natural disaster. Spontaneous prayer is whatever we need it to be.

We do not try to change God through prayer; rather, we ask for the strength for ourselves and others to meet the challenges of life. Through prayer we acknowledge our dependence on God in all things. We remember that God is always with us.

Spontaneous, heartfelt prayer is important in the faith life of all Christians. It must be learned by example. It must be done with love.

Prayer Checklist

Using a prayer checklist helps children think about when, where, how, and why they pray. Ask the children to check the statements that are true for them.

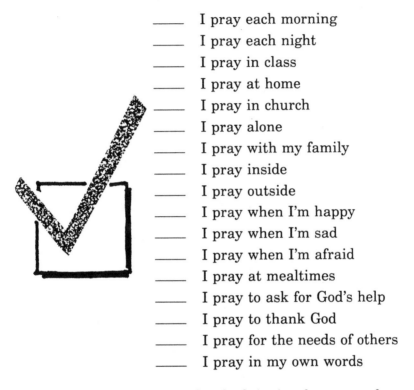

_____ I pray each morning

_____ I pray each night

_____ I pray in class

_____ I pray at home

_____ I pray in church

_____ I pray alone

_____ I pray with my family

_____ I pray inside

_____ I pray outside

_____ I pray when I'm happy

_____ I pray when I'm sad

_____ I pray when I'm afraid

_____ I pray at mealtimes

_____ I pray to ask for God's help

_____ I pray to thank God

_____ I pray for the needs of others

_____ I pray in my own words

When the children have finished, invite them to make comments about each area of prayer. Children can learn from one another through a discussion of this kind. This checklist also reminds the children that there are many times and reasons to pray to God.

Prayer in Parts

Traditional prayers, such as the Our Father, can be prayed in parts to allow the students to focus on specific lines. This helps the students concentrate on the meaning of the prayer.

Provide a copy of the prayer for each student with the parts marked. Designate the left side of the room group 1, the middle group 2, and the right side group 3.

Group 1: Our Father,
who art in heaven,

Group 2: hallowed be thy name;

Group 3: thy kingdom come;
thy will be done on earth
as it is in heaven.

Group 1: Give us this day our daily bread;

Group 2: and forgive us our trespasses as we
forgive those who trespass against us

Group 3: and lead us not into temptation,
but deliver us from evil.

All: Amen.

Taking the prayer apart like this helps the students see it in a new light. They do not rush through it so fast, but instead concentrate more on what the prayer is saying. Praying in parts is helpful to both students and adults.

Hail Mary
With Gestures

Using gestures with the Hail Mary helps students become totally involved in this prayer. Gestures help them express their thoughts and feelings as well as the words. Gestures for this prayer follow.*

Hail Mary	*(Right hand extended upward left.)*
Full of grace	*(Cross arms over chest, head lowered.)*
The Lord is with you	*(Head back, arms in circular movement out and up.)*
Blessed are you	*(Arms straight out, slightly to sides, palms extended.)*
Among women	*(One hand crossed over other, about waist high.)*
And blessed is the fruit of your womb, Jesus	*(Arms in cradle position.)*
Holy Mary	*(Arms extended outward, palms up, reaching out, step forward on left foot.)*
Mother of God	*(Circle downward slowly.)*
Pray for us sinners, now	*(Hands folded in prayer.)*
And at the hour of our death	*(Down to one knee, hands extended toward back.)*
Amen	*(Stand, arms extended, palms up, chest high.)*

These gestures help students understand this special prayer and pray it more fully. Through the use of gestures, students find new meaning in a familiar prayer.

Music

It is important to encourage the children to pray with music. Children and music go together; music appeals to all kinds of children. God gave us the gift of music to enjoy and to use in prayer. Music helps us lift up our minds and our hearts to God. Music enables children to celebrate God's presence together in a joyful way.

Songs written especially for children are the best to use in the classroom. These are songs that use words children understand and that express ideas using images with which children are familiar. The catchy tunes of children's songs are easy for children to learn and remember.

Music can be woven into the classroom in many different ways. Part of the class time can be set aside to help the children learn a song. Several classes can come together to sing songs and praise God with their voices. Songs can begin and end prayer services done with children, or a song on tape can serve as a meditation to help students focus their thoughts on God. Such meditations also allow the children to hear God speaking to their hearts.

Songs based on the Bible are very meaningful. Look up the original verses in the Bible and discuss the meaning of the song. Music can be a part of the children's experience and lives in many ways. Most important, music can help children pray.

I Can Pray Action Rhyme

Action rhymes are great learning activities for children. Rhymes help children participate in the class and understand the message better. The following action rhyme helps children to grasp the idea that there are many ways to pray.* Invite all the children to do the actions.

I can kneel, I can stand,
   (Kneel, then stand.)
I can stretch up tall.
   (Raise arms above head.)
I can pray in so many ways,
   (Point to fingers one at a time.)
I know God hears them all.
   (Nod head and smile.)

I can fold my hands to pray,
   (Fold hands.)
I can spread them wide.
   (Open palms, arms outstretched.)
I can pray so many ways,
   (Point to fingers one at a time.)
And still God's by my side.
   (Nod head and smile.)

I can dance, I can sing,
   (Dance around, pretend to sing.)
I can whisper low.
   (Pretend to whisper.)
I can pray so many ways,
   (Point to fingers one at a time.)
God always hears, I know!
   (Nod head and smile.)

This type of action rhyme shows children as well as tells them about prayer. It enables them to be active learners and helps them remember what they learn for a longer period of time. Action rhymes help make learning about prayer an interesting experience for children.

Thank-You Daisy

God made the world out of love for us, and it contains many wondrous gifts. Children respond to God with thanksgiving when they become aware of all that God has done for us. Discuss with the children some of the things that God has made, such as birds, fish, pets, animals, flowers, rivers, trees, mountains, sunshine, friends, parents, and grandparents. All these are expressions of God's love.

One way to help children praise God for these gifts is with a thank-you daisy. This is a construction paper flower with five yellow petals, an orange center, and a green stem and leaves. Help the children cut all of the pieces out of construction paper.

Then tell them to print "Thank you, God" on the orange center of their flower. Next they print something for which they are thankful on each petal. Remind the children of the things discussed in class, but let them know that they can print whatever they like. This helps the students personalize their thank-you daisy.

When they have finished, help them arrange their flower on a blue background sheet. Then they can glue all the pieces in place. The children can take home the flowers or display them on the bulletin board as a reminder of God's goodness to us. A thank-you daisy helps children express thanksgiving to God for the many gifts God has given them.

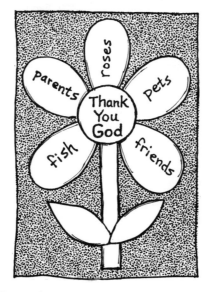

G-R-E-A-T
Prayer Formula

Many students find it difficult to pray in their own words. One way to help them is to give them a prayer formula as a guide to writing their own prayers.* This helps personalize prayer for them. Begin by composing a class prayer together before asking students to write their own individual prayers.

The G-R-E-A-T prayer formula stands for the five sections of the prayer:

> **G**reeting
>
> **R**eason
>
> **E**motion
>
> **A**ction
>
> **T**hanks

The first step is the greeting. Address God in a familiar way, for example, as Father.

The second part is the reason. State the reason for praying, such as needing help or giving thanks for blessings.

The third part is the emotion. Explain to God how we feel, for example, worried, happy, afraid.

The fourth part is the action. Ask God for what we want, such as good health or help with a specific problem.

The last part is thanks. Give thanks for all God's help — past, present, and future.

Here is a sample G-R-E-A-T prayer:

> Loving Father,
>
> We ask for your help.

We are afraid and anxious
　　because Dad is going into
　　the hospital next week.
Please be with him and
　　make him well.
Thank you for your love
　　now and always. Amen.

This type of structured prayer format helps students know where to begin in composing their own prayers. They can use the formula and later learn to talk to God in their own words without it.

Class Prayers

A great idea that involves the children in the class is asking them to bring in prayers. At each class ask for a volunteer to provide the class prayer for the following class. Send home a reminder note to the parents so they can help the student select a prayer and remember to bring it in.

The prayer should be the student's choice. It can be a traditional prayer, a prayer the child wrote, the prayer of a saint, a prayer from the Bible, or whatever the student chooses to share with the class.

This idea provides a wide variety of prayer experiences for the class. Children may select prayers that the teacher had not thought about using. This idea helps the students feel that they are contributing members of the group. It allows them to take responsibility for their own learning.

Toward the end of the school year usually even the shy students will feel secure and confident enough to volunteer to bring in a prayer. This is a great step forward for them.

Letting the students select the class prayers helps provide prayers that are meaningful to the class. Let the students choose whether to read the prayer themselves or have the teacher read it to the class. Class prayers help the students learn to pray together and to pray in many different ways.

Psalm Prayer

The psalms of the Bible are beautiful sources of prayer. The 150 psalms show a variety of prayer forms. Some of the psalms are prayers of thanksgiving to God and are suitable for children's prayer. For example, divide Psalm 100 into parts and ask for volunteers to read.

Reader 1: Sing joyfully to the LORD, all you lands;

Reader 2: serve the LORD with gladness;
come before him with joyful song.

Reader 3: Know that the LORD is God;
he made us, his we are;
his people, the flock he tends.

Reader 4: Enter his gates with thanksgiving,
his courts with praise;

Reader 5: Give thanks to him; bless his name,
for he is good;

the LORD, whose kindness endures forever,

and his faithfulness, to all generations.

This lovely psalm reminds us that we are people of God and that our God is deserving of prayers and praise. This psalm helps us put into words what is in our hearts and can help students realize that prayer can be a joyful experience.

Sign of the Cross Badge

The first memorized prayer that most children learn is the sign of the cross. This is both a prayer and a call to prayer. It is a sign of our belief in the Trinity. The cross also reminds us of Jesus' love for us and his call to follow him.

This important prayer can be learned by young children. Talk with them about times they have seen others use this prayer — upon entering and leaving church, when being blessed at mass, at baptisms, and before and after prayer.

It is important to stand side by side with the children when teaching them to make the sign of the cross. Otherwise they will see a mirror image and do it backward.

When the children have learned to make the sign of the cross, make badges for them to wear home. Cut purple cross shapes out of construction paper and print on them the words "Sign of the Cross." Then put double-stick tape on the back of each one so that they will stick to the children's clothing. Be sure all the children receive their badges on the same day, even if some must be given extra help learning this prayer.

Young children are proud to wear home their sign of the cross badges. They are eager to explain the meaning and show parents and others their new skill. These badges turn a feat of memorization into a special time for the children. They will be eager to make the sign of the cross when they pray at home or at church.

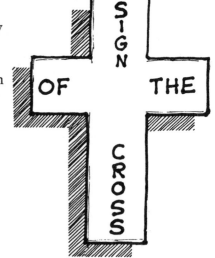

Our Father Meditation

Sometimes students have difficulty understanding the meaning of traditional prayers such as the Our Father. Taking the prayer line by line in a prayer service can help students discover its meaning. Everyone can participate in saying the words of the Our Father; in addition, several students can read the other sections.

All: **Our father, who art in heaven,**

Reader 1: God, we call you our Father as Jesus taught us.

All: **Hallowed be thy name.**

Reader 2: We honor you as Creator of our world and all good things in it.

All: **Thy kingdom come:**

Reader 3: May we show your presence to everyone we meet.

All: **Thy will be done on earth as it is in heaven.**

Reader 4: Send your Spirit to direct our lives as you would have us live them.

All: **Give us this day our daily bread**

Reader 5: Help us to remember that everything we have is a gift from you.

All: **And forgive us our trespasses**

Reader 6: We ask your help to start anew each time we falter.

All: **As we forgive those who trespass against us.**

Reader 7: May we always readily forgive those who hurt us.

All: **And lead us not into temptation, but deliver us from evil.**

Reader 8: Be with us in everything we do.

All: **Amen.**

The easiest way to do this prayer is to make copies for everyone in the class. Put an asterisk by the reading parts on separate pages. Then give those to the students who volunteer.

Students sometimes ask why Catholics do not add the doxology — "For thine is the kingdom, and the power, and the glory forever and ever" — at the end of the Our Father. The answer is that this is not how the prayer is recorded in the Bible either in Matthew 6:9–13 or in Luke 11:2–4. It apparently was added to some early translations by a scribe.

We do, nevertheless, include the doxology at mass as a separate prayer. This was apparently done in early times, since the doxology is a prayer of worship.

Rewriting Prayers

Another way to help students understand the words and ideas of traditional prayers is to let them rewrite a prayer. In this way they can begin to see what the prayer really says.

Go through the Hail Mary with them line by line and talk about unfamiliar words. Then rewrite it. The prayer may turn out something like this:

> We honor you, Mary,
>
> because God is with you.
>
> You are special and
>
> were chosen to be
>
> the mother of Jesus.
>
> Blessed Mary,
>
> mother of God's Son,
>
> pray for us always.
>
> Amen.

Helping the children understand the meaning of this prayer helps them pray it more fully. The students can all contribute their ideas, which can lead to a discussion not only about the prayer, but about the importance of Mary as a model in our lives. Rewriting prayers is very helpful to students.

Prayer Card

Children can make prayer cards as reminders to pray each day. Make the prayer cards from pieces of colored posterboard cut into rectangles 7" by 10". Fold the posterboard piece in half at the 5" point to make a stand up card.

Have the students print a line from a favorite prayer on the front of the card on the right-hand side. Then, on the left side, illustrate the prayer with colorful markers.

For example, students studying the Our Father could print the first part of that prayer on their card: "Our Father, who art in heaven, hallowed be thy name." As an illustration a student might draw the sun coming out from behind a cloud, emphasizing the role of God as Creator. The prayer contains many images. The choice of what and how to illustrate the prayer should be left to the individual student.

Ask the students to take the card home and display it in a suitable place, such as the dinner table, as a call to pray together. This project helps students reflect on the meaning of prayers that they know. It is also a reminder to pray. Prayer cards extend the learning from the classroom into the home, where the faith is lived.

Prayer Partners

Prayer is an integral part of who we are as Christians. We are called to be people of prayer. Children should learn to pray not only for their own needs, but also for the needs of others. We are to be a community of God's people, who care about one another. Part of showing concern for other people is praying for them and their intentions. One way to encourage prayer for others is through prayer partners.

Discuss with the children why prayers for other people are important. Stress that we are all members of God's family. Ask the children to print their names on pieces of paper and put them into a basket. Then each child draws the name of a child to be his or her prayer partner.

When the class prayer is concluded for the day, ask the children to each offer a moment of silent prayer for the person whose name they have drawn. Encourage them to pray for the needs of that child at home during the coming week also. Ask them to pray for their prayer partner by name and ask that God will give the person the strength to face the challenges in his or her life.

The prayer partners project helps students learn to pray for the needs of others. It also fosters a sense of community within the classroom. The children not only pray for their own prayer partners, but they know that someone is praying for them and their needs as well.

Blessings

The custom of blessings is one that comes to us over thousands of years. There are many types of blessings that are important in our lives as Catholics. We receive a blessing at mass, infants are blessed by parents and godparents at the beginning of the baptism ceremony, we ask a blessing when we sit down to eat a meal. Through blessings we call upon God and ask him to guide us and be with us.

Blessings are a way of proclaiming our belief in God and affirming other people. Blessings make God's love more personal. They help us show our care and concern for one another.

A lovely blessing is found in Numbers 6:24–26. It can be used as a closing prayer by a teacher at the end of class or the end of the year:

> The LORD bless you and keep you!
> The LORD let his face shine upon
> you, and be gracious to you!
> The LORD look upon you kindly and
> give you peace!

This blessing lets the students feel God's love for them and know that the teacher wishes the best for them. It connects us with all those who have used this blessing through the centuries. This blessing also reminds the students as they leave the classroom that God is here with us and that we should ask for God's help in all things.

Chapter 6

We Are Called to Celebrate

The seasons of the church year help us to remember all that God has done for us. Together we are called to celebrate the birth, life, death, and resurrection of Jesus Christ. Through the symbols and traditions of the liturgical seasons we are reminded of what it is that we believe as Christians and who we are called to be.

The season of Advent is the four weeks before Christmas. It is a time of preparation for the coming of Jesus — past, present, and future. We remember how Jesus came into the world long ago, we seek his presence in our lives now, and we look forward to his coming again at the end of time.

The Christmas season celebrates the birth of Jesus in a stable in Bethlehem. God loved us so much that he sent us his only Son. Jesus shared our humanity so that we could share his divinity. Jesus is the Word of God present here among us. We should give glory to God as the angels did on the first Christmas. The season continues until the feast of the Baptism of the Lord.

Lent is the season of preparation for the great feast of Easter. It lasts forty days, mirroring the forty days that Jesus spend in the desert preparing for his public ministry. It is a time when we are called to prayer, fasting, and almsgiving. As we journey toward Easter we are to turn away from selfishness and toward the light of Christ. During Lent we remember our baptismal promises and seek to live them in our lives. We reflect on how God calls us to life with him.

The Easter season is the summit of the church year. We celebrate together the resurrection of Jesus Christ and the new life he brings to all of us. The fifty days from Easter to Pentecost are a time of proclaiming the good news of Jesus Christ to others as the apostles did. The feast of Pentecost reminds us that the Holy Spirit is at work in our lives and our church.

Studying the seasons of the church year can help children begin to understand what faith in Jesus Christ is all about. In celebrating the liturgical seasons together we reflect on the life and message of Jesus Christ and how we are to live. We are called as a community of God's people to journey to the Father, through his Son, Jesus Christ, with the help of the Holy Spirit.

Advent Jesse Tree

A children's liturgy for Advent is a meaningful way to celebrate this special season in the church year. One way to carry out the Advent themes of waiting and hope is by incorporating a Jesse tree ceremony into the liturgy. This ceremony can also be done as part of a prayer service.

Twelve students have special parts in this ceremony. The teacher acts as the narrator. The students make appropriate symbols for the Jesse tree out of posterboard. Use a potted tree branch as the tree on which the symbols are hung during the liturgy.

It is helpful to put each part on an index card. The students can try to memorize the words, but should bring the index card with them just in case. At the beginning of the ceremony all the students involved gather near the tree. One at a time students step forward to say their parts and then place a symbol on the tree. Here is the ceremony.

The Jesse Tree*

Narrator: Advent is a time of waiting for the birthday of Jesus. We all love to get ready for birthdays. We celebrate them with family and friends. Christmas is Jesus birthday. We will get ready by decorating Jesus' family tree, the Jesse tree. Jesse was the father of King David, one of the ancestors of Jesus. We will decorate the Jesse Tree with ornaments that reminded us of the people who waited for Jesus to come.

Adam with Eve: I am Adam and this is my wife, Eve. We are the first man and woman. It is to us that God made his promise to send Jesus. Our symbol is an apple with a bite out of it.

Noah: I am Noah. God saved me, my family, and many animals from the flood. My symbol is the ark.

Abraham:	I am Abraham. God chose me to be the father of his special people. Because I trusted God when he asked me to sacrifice my son, Isaac, God blessed me with many children who would wait for the coming of Jesus. My symbol is a dagger and a bundle of sticks.
Joseph:	I am Joseph, Abraham's great-grandson. When I was young, my brothers sold me as a slave in Egypt. Later, I was set free, became governor, and helped God's people when there was no food in their home-land. When Jesus comes, he will save all people. My symbol is a many-colored coat.
Moses:	I am Moses. I led God's people out of Egypt. I re-ceived ten commandments from him for his people. My symbol is the tablets of stone that God's laws were written on.
Jesse:	I am Jesse, David's father. Jesus was from the root of Jesse. Jesus' family tree grew and grew. Many people waited for his coming. My symbol is a tree.
David:	I am David. I am a king who loved God very much. I wrote many psalms, the songs you pray or sing at mass. I came from Bethlehem where Jesus would be born many years later. My symbol is a crown.
Solomon:	I am Solomon. I am a king, too. I built a great church, called the Temple, where God's people could come to worship him. My symbol is the temple.
Jonah:	I am Jonah. When I did not obey God, he sent a great fish to carry me to the place I was to go. I was in the fish three days as Jesus would be in the grave three days. My symbol is a whale.
Joseph:	I am Joseph, the husband of the virgin Mary and foster father of Jesus. Since I was a carpenter, my symbol is a saw and hammer.
Mary:	I am Mary. God chose me to be the mother of Jesus, the Savior that everyone waited for. My symbol is a lily because God let me be born without any sins.

Narrator: About 2,000 years ago Jesus was born in Bethlehem. We rejoice that he has come. We wait and get ready now to celebrate that wonderful day again in our hearts and prepare for him to come.

This ceremony helps the students understand how the people waited thousands of years for Jesus to come. They kept hope alive by believing in the promise of God. We too need to keep hope alive in our hearts during the season of Advent.

Come, Lord Jesus

The following Advent choral reading helps students learn and express what this season means.

Solo 1:   During Advent we prepare our hearts and our homes for Christmas.

All: **Come, Lord Jesus.**

Solo 2:   We share the joy of the season by reaching out to help other people.

All: **Come, Lord Jesus.**

Solo 3:   Advent is a time of waiting and hope.

All: **Come, Lord Jesus.**

Solo 4:   We wait for four weeks as our ancestors in faith waited thousands of years for a savior.

All: **Come, Lord Jesus.**

Solo 5:   God loves us so much that he sent his only Son to us.

All: **Come, Lord Jesus.**

Solo 6:   We celebrate his coming with praise and thanksgiving.

All: **Come, Lord Jesus.**

This choral reading involves all the students in the class. It can be used as part of an Advent program or as a classroom prayer.

Prayer to Mary

Advent is a time of prayer. One type of prayer calls upon the intercession of the saints, especially Mary. We ask her to pray for us to God. We also see in her life an example of the way we should live. These ideas are reflected in the following prayer to Mary, which can be used as a class meditation during the season of Advent:

Mary, Sign of Hope*

O Mary, whenever we remember you
　　and call upon your name,
we feel hope in us and long to know
　　with you the Emmanuel —
　　the experience of God's nearness.
We thank you for your fervent prayer,
　　for your longing that was fulfilled
　　in the coming of the Savior.
Pray for us, that our lives
　　may be a constant thanksgiving
　　for his coming and become for many
　　a sign of hope, of trust,
　　and an invitation to seek the Lord. Amen.

Mary is indeed a model of hope for all of us during the Advent season and always. This prayer reminds us of what Advent is about.

Children's Song

Young children love to sing. One way to help them understand the season of Advent is through a children's song. Sing the words to the tune of "London Bridge."* Have the children follow the teacher's lead in doing appropriate motions to fit the words of the song while they sing.

This is the way we trim the tree,
trim the tree, trim the tree.
This is the way we trim the tree
to get ready for Christmas morning.

This is the way we help other people,
help other people, help other people.
This is the way we help other people
to get ready for Christmas morning.

This is the way we wrap our gifts,
wrap our gifts, wrap our gifts.
This is the way we wrap our gifts
to get ready for Christmas morning.

This is the way we say our prayers,
say our prayers, say our prayers.
This is the way we say our prayers
to get ready for Christmas morning.

This is the way we hang the wreath,
hang the wreath, hang the wreath.
This is the way we hang the wreath
to get ready for Christmas morning.

This is the way we show our love,
show our love, show our love.
This is the way we show our love
to get ready for Christmas morning.

This song reminds the children that the things we do during Advent are preparations for the feast of Christmas. We not only decorate our homes during this time, but we show care for others too. Giving to others is a more outward focus than concentrating on what we will receive.

Christmas Acrostic

In an acrostic each letter of the key word is used as the beginning letter of another word. The students will enjoy composing acrostics in which each word relates in some way to the Christmas season.

Give each student a sheet of manila paper. Have them print the word CHRISTMAS vertically down the left side of the paper with a red marker. Then ask them to think of a Christmas word for each letter. Help them with letters they find difficult. They can use green markers for the words.

Here is a sample Christmas acrostic:

C hrist child
H olly
R edeemer
I cicles
S t. Nicholas
T ree
M ary
A ngel
S tar

This acrostic is both fun and a challenge. It helps students think of the many facets of our celebration of this season.

Mosaic Tree

A great craft for children during this time of year is a mosaic Christmas tree. The only materials needed for this project are construction paper, scissors, glue, and a marker.

Have the students draw a Christmas tree shape on a sheet of green construction paper. (Some students may need to use a pattern to trace the tree shape with the marker.) Then have the children print *Merry Christmas* underneath the tree.

Next the students should cut out small squares of construction paper in a variety of colors — red, yellow, green, orange, and purple. The squares can be glued on the tree in any arrangement that pleases the students. The squares can overlap one another. Even young children can decorate a Christmas tree using this method.

Children are happy with how the tree looks when they are finished. Each tree is different because of the colors used and the arrangement of the mosaic squares. These colorfully decorated Christmas trees can be taken home and displayed as a sign of the season. This project is fun and helps the children see Christmas as a joyful time.

Traditions Booklet

Children enjoy making gifts for their parents during the Christmas season. An inexpensive and meaningful gift is a Christmas traditions booklet.

Send a note home with each child asking the parents to contribute an idea, custom, recipe, prayer, or craft for the Christmas season. Type each submission. (Do not put the names of those submitting the ideas because some families will not participate and the children could be embarrassed.)

Duplicate the ideas on half-sheets of colored paper. On the cover page have the children write a Christmas greeting for their families. Provide stickers and markers so they can decorate the pages. Then show the students how to assemble the pages and staple them together on the left-hand side to form booklets.

You can expect families to contribute ideas such as,

> Christmas meal prayer
>
> Stained-glass cookie recipe
>
> Tree decorating party
>
> Homemade ornament craft
>
> Ethnic customs
>
> Neighborhood caroling activity
>
> Recipe for hot cider
>
> Praying for senders of Christmas cards
>
> Visiting a senior day-care center

This booklet is a lovely gift for parents. It is one of those gifts that keeps on giving. The ideas included in it help families celebrate the season together.

Las Posadas

The Hispanic tradition of *Las Posadas* ("the dwellings") is a lovely one for children. This custom centers on acting out Mary and Joseph's search for a place to stay in Bethlehem. The children go from classroom to classroom on their journey. This is an excellent way to help children remember the meaning of the Christmas season.

The children begin in their own classroom with an introduction. Then they walk in procession down the hallway with two children representing Mary and Joseph leading the way.

At each classroom the children serenade those inside with a Christmas carol. Appropriate songs include "O Little Town of Bethlehem," "O Come All Ye Faithful," "Away in a Manger," and "Silent Night." Then Mary and Joseph ask if there is room for them to stay. (Instruct the teachers ahead of time to say that there is not.) The children proceed to the next door. At each door they sing a carol, ask for admittance, and are turned away.

Finally, when the children reach the last class, they are told that there is room for Mary and Joseph to spend the night. They all are invited inside. Have the children gather around a nativity scene and hear the story of the first Christmas from Luke's gospel. Remind the children that each of us must make room in our life for Jesus during the busy Christmas season because this is what Christmas is all about.

Then have the children sing "Joy to the World," and serve refreshments.

The custom of *Las Posadas* is a great way for children to understand the Christmas story. It helps them to celebrate the coming of Jesus into the world and our lives.

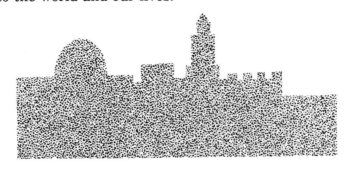

Nativity Display

Children need to be reminded of the true meaning of our Christmas celebration. One way to do this is to help the children make a nativity display for their homes.

Each child needs a half-sheet of construction paper. Fold it in half and crease with the two sides meeting. Next, trim the top into a rounded arc. Then have the children open up the paper and lay it flat.

On a small sheet of white paper have each child copy Luke 2:7 from the Bible or provide a typewritten copy:

And she gave birth to her firstborn son. She wrapped him in swaddling clothes and laid him in a manger, because there was no room for them in the inn (Lk 2:7).

Each child should glue the Christmas story to the left side of his or her paper. Then, from old Christmas cards with nativity scenes, have the children cut out a manger scene to glue on the right side of their paper. This provides a colorful illustration for the Christmas story. The children can add a gold star as a finishing touch.

This nativity display is a reminder of the Christmas season for the child who makes it and all those who see it displayed.

Epiphany Prayer

The celebration of the feast of Epiphany is the climax of the Christmas season. Epiphany recounts the journey of the magi. It helps us remember that Jesus is the light of the world, and we are to follow him. We are to search for him in our lives just as the magi did in theirs. We want to help the students understand that Epiphany is a celebration for all people because Jesus came for all of us. Use the following Epiphany prayer in class.*

> God of the Universe,
> Our dreams keep us going and help us
>   to rise above everyday problems,
>   to keep our eyes on you and all that is good.
> Help us to follow your star
>   in our dreams,
>   and to give you the gift of ourselves
>   every day of our lives.
> Thank you for dreams
>   and stars
>   and all that you have given us
>   to help us to follow you.
> Amen.

This prayer helps us to remember that the best gift that the wise men brought was the gift of themselves. They kept on searching until they found Jesus present in their lives. Thus their hope became reality.

Lenten Intention

The season of Lent is a time to stop and look at how we can more closely follow Jesus. It is helpful for children to pick out one thing in particular to work on during this time. A Lenten intention helps children focus their thoughts on acting in the spirit of Jesus in their lives.

First, talk in class in a general way about the kinds of things that can be Lenten intentions. Also give the students some specific examples. Encourage them to participate in this discussion with ideas they might have heard of or tried in previous years.

Provide a Lenten intention paper for each student — a half-sheet of purple paper titled "Lenten Intention" with these words duplicated on it, "During Lent I will _____ in order to show my love for Jesus and get ready to celebrate Easter." Provide another blank line at the bottom for the student to sign his or her name. On the left show a cross as a reminder of following Jesus and the words from Ash Wednesday: "Turn away from sin and be faithful to the gospel."

Encourage the students to think of a Lenten intention for themselves this year, one that will help them be faithful to Jesus' teachings in the gospels. Examples of Lenten intentions that students have chosen are:

> Do my chores without being asked
> Say an extra prayer each day
> Help my dad take out the trash
> Read the Bible
> Pray before I go to sleep
> Help my parents
> Take my dog for a walk
> Help my mom set the table
> Say grace at dinnertime
> Be nice to a friend I do not like
> Stop fighting with my sister
> Make my own lunch
> Share a toy with my brother

Children should not be asked to share their Lenten intentions with others. Instead, have the students roll them up and tie them with purple yarn. Then all the intentions can be put into a basket. Have the intentions brought forward during a children's liturgy or prayer service as an offering to God during the season of Lent.

Lenten Intention

During Lent I will _____

_____

in order to show my love for Jesus and get ready to

celebrate Easter.

✝   _____

                                              Signed

Choral Reading

A choral reading involves all the students in the class. It is both a message and a prayer. This Lenten choral reading is appropriate for a class prayer service or as part of a Lenten program.

Solo 1:   We are reminded on Ash Wednesday that we are to turn away from sin and be faithful to the gospel.

All: **During Lent we follow the way of Jesus.**

Solo 2:   Jesus said to love God with all our hearts and all our minds.

All: **During Lent we follow the way of Jesus.**

Solo 3:   We must be people of prayer, who praise God with our words and our lives.

All: **During Lent we follow the way of Jesus.**

Solo 4:   Jesus told us to love one another as we love ourselves.

All: **During Lent we follow the way of Jesus.**

Solo 5:   We must be people who care for others and who see each person we meet as God's creation.

All: **During Lent we follow the way of Jesus.**

Solo 6:   We must reach out to those in need and remember the words of Jesus: "As long as you did it for the least of my brothers, you did it for me."

All: **During Lent we follow the way of Jesus.**

Solo 7:   These forty days are a time to let go of selfish ways of living and instead to embrace the presence of God in our lives.

All: **During Lent we follow the way of Jesus.**

Solo 8:   God loves us so much that he sent his only Son to us.

All: **During Lent we follow the way of Jesus.**

Solo 9:   Jesus died for us so that we might have new life through him.

All: **During Lent we follow the way of Jesus.**

Solo 10:   We will celebrate the resurrection of Jesus at Easter as we are all made new in him.

All: **During Lent we follow the way of Jesus.**

A choral reading requires no memorization because the parts are read. It is a way of expressing what we believe in words and of reminding others what Lent means to us as Christians.

Symbol Table

A display of symbols associated with the Lenten season can help students recall what this time means to Christians. A symbol table can be set up in the hallway, classroom, or chapel during Lent.

Cover a table with a purple cloth. On the table arrange these items:

Cross

Open Bible

Bowl of ashes

Rice bowl container

Crown of thorns

Three large nails

Artificial grapes

Stalk of wheat

Plant

Add other appropriate symbols that are meaningful to the children and part of the parish observance of Lent if you wish. The Bible should be open to one of the accounts of the passion.

This display does not need words or explanations. All those who pass will see the symbols. The items on the table speak in different ways to different people. The symbol table is a constant reminder of the season of Lent and Christ's journey to the Father.

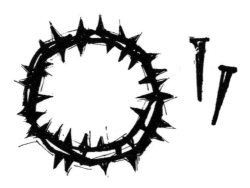

Cross Banner

A wonderful craft for the Lenten season is to make individual cross banners. The students can hang the banners at home as a reminder to follow Jesus.

Each student needs a 7" by 9" piece of green felt for the banner. Fold the top inch over to make a rod pocket and glue it along the edge. (Craft glue does not soak through the felt and gives a better finished product.)

While the glue is drying, have the students cut out 6" by 5" crosses from purple felt. (A sharp scissors is essential in working with felt.) Purple is the traditional color of Lent and is very appropriate for these banners. Many different shapes of crosses can be used. The cross should be glued to the center of the banner.

Next, cut small triangles of four different colors from felt for accents. Bright colors such as yellow, red, white, and blue look good. Glue one piece onto each section of the cross.

To finish the banner have the students insert an 8" wooden dowel through the top. They can tie a 16" piece of purple yarn to both ends of the dowel to use as a hanger.

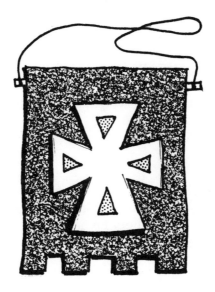

Holy Week Retreat

A retreat helps students understand the meaning of Holy Week. Hold the retreat on the Saturday before Holy Week begins or on the day the schools dismiss for Easter break. Devote four hours, one hour each, to exploring Palm Sunday, Holy Thursday, Good Friday, and the Easter Vigil. By doing all of this on the same day, the students are immersed in the Holy Week experience and can see more clearly how each day fits into the whole week.

The first hour is about Palm Sunday. Present an introduction to Holy Week to all the students. Then divide them into age groups to hear the story of Palm Sunday and discuss it. Follow the discussion with a craft project, such as making paper palms or folding a palm into a cross.

The second hour is the study of Holy Thursday, which begins the Triduum. The Triduum lasts from sunset on Holy Thursday to sunset on Easter Sunday. During these three days we celebrate the death and resurrection of Jesus Christ. During the session on Holy Thursday, read the story of the Last Supper from the Bible and talk about the eucharist in their lives. Have some groups work on a crossword puzzle, while others share a meal of bread and grape juice.

The third hour explores Good Friday. Have one of the older classes present the stations of the cross. Then have the students discuss why we call the day Jesus died Good Friday. Finish by having the students make twig crosses bound with yarn or mosaic crosses out of construction paper.

The final hour of the Holy Week retreat celebrates the Easter Vigil. Discuss the symbols of fire, water, and light. Give the students the opportunity to renew their baptismal promises as part of a prayer service. Then either decorate candles or make stained-glass windows out of paper.

A Holy Week retreat is a wonderful way for students to explore the meaning of Holy Week for us as Christians and to celebrate it in their own lives. It also helps them be better prepared to participate in the parish celebration of Holy Week.

Easter Symbols

There are many signs and symbols that we use during the Easter season in our churches, our classrooms, and our homes. These symbols help us express what we are celebrating and what we believe as Christians. The symbols have value, though, only if we understand what they represent.

Paschal candle.   Lit at the Easter vigil, the candle is a sign that Jesus is the light of the world whom we are to follow. It is lit on each Sunday of Easter until Pentecost.

Hot cross buns.   These special treats have a cross made on the top of each bun with white icing. The fruit-filled buns are a sign of life and love. God loved us so much that he sent his only Son to us.

Easter eggs.   Eggs remind us of the new life that Jesus brings. Chicks hatch from eggs and thus eggs are a sign of the new life of springtime. Other baby animals, like ducklings and bunnies, are also born in the spring and have thus become associated with Easter.

Lamb.   Cakes in the shape of a lamb are a symbol of Jesus as the Passover Lamb. At the time when lambs were being killed for the Passover meal, Jesus was handed over to be crucified. He was sacrificed as the true Passover Lamb for all of us.

Empty tomb.   The tomb symbolizes Christ's resurrection on the first Easter. It was actually the presence of the risen Christ among them that convinced his followers that he was indeed risen. Paul notes in 1 Corinthians that Jesus was seen by more than five hundred eyewitnesses after his resurrection. Later the empty tomb came to be a resurrection symbol.

Easter lily.   This flower is a symbol of Jesus Christ because it grows in darkness from a bulb into a flowering plant. Jesus also arose from the darkness of death into new life. The white Easter lily and white church decorations remind us of the new creation.

Butterfly.   This beautiful creature can help us understand the resurrection. Just as a caterpillar emerges from a cocoon as a beautiful butterfly, so Jesus was transformed on his journey from death to life. All of us will make this journey.

Ask the children to name other signs and symbols of the Easter season that they have seen. Discuss with them the meaning of the symbols and customs so that they can understand how they relate to Easter. In this way the signs of Easter will help the children remember that it is a celebration of Christ's resurrection and the new life he brings to all of us.

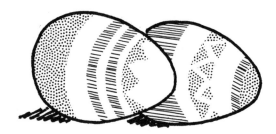

Alleluia Cards

Easter greeting cards handmade by children are wonderful to give away at Easter time. As people of the resurrection we express the true meaning of the season when we share the good news with others.

Make the cards from sheets of white or pastel copy paper and markers. Fold each sheet of paper in half to make a card. On the front of the card have the students print "Alleluia" and draw a picture of something associated with the Easter season.

On the inside of the card each student prints an appropriate Bible verse that expresses the joy of Easter. Write verses on the board for students to copy. Of course, allow them to choose a different verse if they wish. Some verses to suggest are:

Rejoice in the Lord (Phil 3:1).

Sing to the Lord a new song (Is 42:10).

This is the day the Lord has made (Ps 118:24).

Thanks be to God (2 Cor 9:15).

Blessed be the Lord (Lk 1:68).

The final step is for the students to sign their name to the card and give it away to someone they choose. In this way they share the joy of the Easter season and the new life Jesus brings with others.

Food Baskets

We can celebrate the joy of Easter by sharing with others. One way to do this is to collect food items for families experiencing financial difficulties. The parish social ministry office or local outreach program is usually willing to collect names of those in need of assistance and to be responsible for distribution. This protects the privacy of the families involved.

Each Easter food basket should contain items for a complete Easter dinner, including the following:

Boxed potatoes	Ham
Canned vegetables	Boxed roll mix
Boxes of gelatin	Cake mix
Powdered milk	Canned frosting
Canned fruit	Easter candy

Often a parish organization will provide money for the hams, the most expensive item for the dinners. Then the children and their families can contribute the other items. Ask for volunteers to package the Easter dinners in cardboard cartons decorated with Easter cutouts. Large families will need more items in their dinner box than small families. Add the hams just before distribution.

Easter food baskets are an excellent way to help other people celebrate Easter. The project is a practical way for families to work together to help one another in the spirit of the Easter season.

Butterfly Banner

A butterfly is one symbol of the resurrection of Jesus Christ. The butterfly represents the new life of Easter, both the new life of springtime and the new life we have because of Jesus.

Children like to make individual butterfly banners to take home and display during the Easter season. Cut a 7" by 9" piece of beige burlap for each child before class. Turn the top inch over and sew before class to make a rod pocket.

Provide sharp scissors, colorful fabric, and a butterfly pattern for designs on the banner. Help the children cut butterfly wings and bodies out of contrasting colors of fabric. Cut letters spelling LIFE from a third color of fabric. (The pieces may need to be precut for young children.)

Tell the children to place the fabric pieces on the banner in any arrangement they wish. The letters can go across the top, the bottom, or the side of the banner. When the pieces are arranged, help them glue them in place with fabric glue.

For the final touch, put an 8" wooden dowel through the rod pocket and tie a 16" piece of green yarn to the dowel ends to form a hanger. Fringe the bottom edge of the banner by pulling individual threads, if desired.

This banner can be displayed throughout the fifty days of the Easter season until Pentecost. It will be a reminder of the new life Jesus Christ brings to us through his life, death, and resurrection.

Road to Emmaus

This echo pantomime helps the students visualize the story of Jesus' appearance to two of his followers after his resurrection. It is based on Luke 24:13–35. The teacher says the words line by line and does the accompanying actions. The students echo the words and motions.

Two followers of Jesus	*(hold up two fingers)*
were walking to Emmaus.	*(walk in place)*
They were talking	*(talking motion with hand)*
about all that had happened.	*(sweep arm side to side)*
While they were talking	*(talking motion with hand)*
Jesus joined them	*(walk in place)*
but they did not know him.	*(shake head no)*
Jesus said to them,	*(finger by mouth)*
"What are you talking about?"	*(hold palms up)*
They told of Jesus' death	*(shake head yes)*
upon a wooden cross	*(make cross shape with finger)*
and how three days later	*(hold up three fingers)*
women found the empty tomb.	*(shrug shoulders)*
Jesus said to the two,	*(finger by mouth)*
"How slow you are to believe	*(hand on heart)*
in what the scriptures say,"	*(hold hands like book)*
The two asked Jesus to stay	*(beckon)*
and eat with them.	*(eating motions)*
So Jesus took the bread,	*(open right hand)*
blessed it, and broke it.	*(pretend to break bread)*
Then the people knew him,	*(hand over eyes, take away)*
but Jesus had left.	*(push hand away from body)*
The two returned to Jerusalem	*(walk in place)*
and told the apostles	*(talking motion with hand)*
all that they had seen.	*(point to eyes)*
They had recognized Jesus	*(hand on heart)*
in the breaking of the bread.	*(nod head)*

The motions help the students understand this Bible story and remember it because the pantomime involves them in the story. This appearance narrative is an important one for students to know because each of us must make our journey to Emmaus and recognize the risen Christ at work in our lives.

Pentecost Prayer

The Easter season comes to an end with the celebration of Pentecost. The Holy Spirit is given to us in our lives as he was to the apostles. We must be open to the Spirit and his gifts.

We must pray that the Spirit fills our lives. The following prayer can be used to help students learn to pray to the Holy Spirit.* It is an appropriate Pentecost prayer. The teacher can act as the leader. A different student should read each petition. Then all the students say the response together.

Leader: Come, Holy Spirit.
Renew the face of the earth.

All: **Come, Holy Spirit.**
Renew the face of the earth.

Reader: Come, Holy Spirit.
Give us the gift of wisdom.

All: **Come, Holy Spirit.**
Renew the face of the earth.

Reader: Come, Holy Spirit.
Give us the gift of courage.

All: **Come, Holy Spirit.**
Renew the face of the earth.

Reader: Come, Holy Spirit.
Give us the gift of understanding.

All: **Come, Holy Spirit.**
Renew the face of the earth.

Reader: Come, Holy Spirit.
Give us the gift of counsel.

All: **Come, Holy Spirit.**
Renew the face of the earth.

Reader: Come, Holy Spirit.
Give us the gift of true knowledge.

All: **Come, Holy Spirit.**
Renew the face of the earth.

Reader: Come, Holy Spirit.
Give us the gift of reverence.

All:	**Come, Holy Spirit.**
	Renew the face of the earth.
Reader:	Come, Holy Spirit.
	Give us the gift of piety.
All:	**Come, Holy Spirit.**
	Renew the face of the earth.
Leader:	Come, Holy Spirit.
	Fill our hearts with your gifts and come upon us as you came upon the disciples on the first Pentecost.
All:	**Amen.**

We are called to live as followers of Jesus through the Spirit. We must help students understand that we are to live as a community of God's people who go out and proclaim that the kingdom of God is present here through the Son. We are to use the talents and abilities given to us by God to share the good news of Jesus Christ with all people. Renewed by the Spirit, we go forth.

Permissions and Acknowledgments:

"If I Were the Church" on page 14 is excerpted from Elaine Ward, *Be and Say a Fingerplay* (Brea, CA: Educational Ministries, Inc., 1982), p. 1.

"Celebrating and Serving" on page 28 is excerpted from *This Is Our Faith: Liturgies and Paraliturgies* by Reverend David Conrad, O.F.M. and Nancy Owen Quinn. © 1987 Silver Burdett & Ginn. All rights reserved. Used with permission.

"Who Is Our Neighbor?" prayer service on page 38 is excerpted from *Gathering Prayers for Children*. Copyright © 1988 by Journal Press II Resources, P.O. Box 744, Cranford, NJ 07016. Permission to reproduce is granted to the subscribing parish/school only. All rights are reserved by law.

The prayer on page 54 is excerpted from James E. Hug S.J., *Scripture Sharing on the Bishop's Economic Pastoral* (Kansas City, MO: Leaven Press, 1985), p. 24.

"Tissue Rainbow Project" on page 61 was adapted from *Blue Ribbon Crafts* by Carol Eide, copyright 1988, Regal Books, Ventura, CA 93003. Used by permission.

"One Little Sheep Is Lost" on page 70 is excerpted from Patricia Brennan-Nichols, *Getting to Know Jesus* (Allen, TX: Tabor Publishing, a division of DLM, Inc., © 1984), pp. 40–41.

"Jesus and Zacchaeus" playlet on page 73 is excerpted from Sisters of Notre Dame, *God Cares for Us* Catechist Manual (Chicago, IL: Loyola University Press, 1980), Theme 9, Session 1.

"Hail Mary With Gestures" on page 101 is excerpted from Robert M. Hamma, ed., *Still More Children's Liturgies* (New York, NY: Paulist Press, 1988), p. 95.

"I Can Pray Action Rhyme" on page 103 is reprinted from 1985 VBS, *God's People Pray*, copyright © 1984 Augsburg Publishing House. Used by permission of Augsburg Fortress.

The idea for the "G-R-E-A-T Prayer Formula" on page 106 is adapted from "A Formula for Writing Prayers," *Notebook For Catechists*, vol. 4, no. 1, p. 10. Copyright © 1984 by Our Sunday Visitor, Inc. Reprinted by permission. All rights reserved.

"The Jesse Tree" on page 119 is excerpted from *Children's Liturgies Made Easy* by Barbara Bartley and Carol Wilson (published in Dubuque, IA: BROWN Publishing-ROA Media, 1989), pp. 34–35. Reprinted with permission.

"Mary, Sign of Hope" on page 123 is excerpted from Bernard Haring, C.SS.R., *Mary and Your Everyday Life* (Liguori, MO: Liguori Publications, 1977), p. 11.

The idea for the "Children's Song" on page 124 is adapted from *Promise* student magazine (Dayton, OH: Pflaum Press, 1986), Volume 1, Number 8.

"Epiphany Prayer" on page 131 is excerpted from Bradley, Peggy, *Advent/Christmas 1987, Family Prayers and Activities*, p. 32 © 1987 Franciscan Communications, Los Angeles, CA.

"Pentecost Prayer" on page 146 is excerpted from *Coming To God's Life* Grade 5 text (New York, NY: William H. Sadlier, Inc., 1988), p. 163.